WHAT YOU NEED TO KNOW ABOUT AI

PROFESSOR BRIAN DAVID JOHNSON
FUTURIST AND AI EXPERT

WHAT YOU NEED TO KNOW ABOUT AI

wren & rook

PROFESSOR BRIAN DAVID JOHNSON
FUTURIST AND AI EXPERT

To you, the reader! Be curious and courageous. The future belongs to you!

First published in Great Britain in 2024 by Wren & Rook

ISBN: 978 1 5263 6678 8

1 3 5 7 9 10 8 6 4 2

MIX
Paper | Supporting
responsible forestry
FSC
www.fsc.org
FSC® C104740

Wren & Rook
An imprint of
Hachette Children's Group
Part of Hodder & Stoughton
Carmelite House
50 Victoria Embankment
London EC4Y 0DZ

An Hachette UK Company
www.hachette.co.uk
www.hachettechildrens.co.uk

Printed and bound in Great Britain by Clays Ltd, Elcograf S.p.A.

‹contents›

Chapter 1:   9
All your AI questions answered

Chapter 2:   49
Gigantic things: Dinosaurs, volcanoes
and the bottom of the ocean

Chapter 3:   73
AI and sport: Putting YOU in the game

Chapter 4:   89
Furry friends and wild animals

Chapter 5:   103
An extraordinary you

Chapter 6:   119
Let's go inside your sentient home

Chapter 7:   135
Robots! Drones! And the machines of
the future!

Chapter 8:   157
Let's go to space!

Chapter 9:   169
Unlimited creativity

Chapter 10:   185
Important stuff: School and jobs

Chapter 11:   197
AI and your future

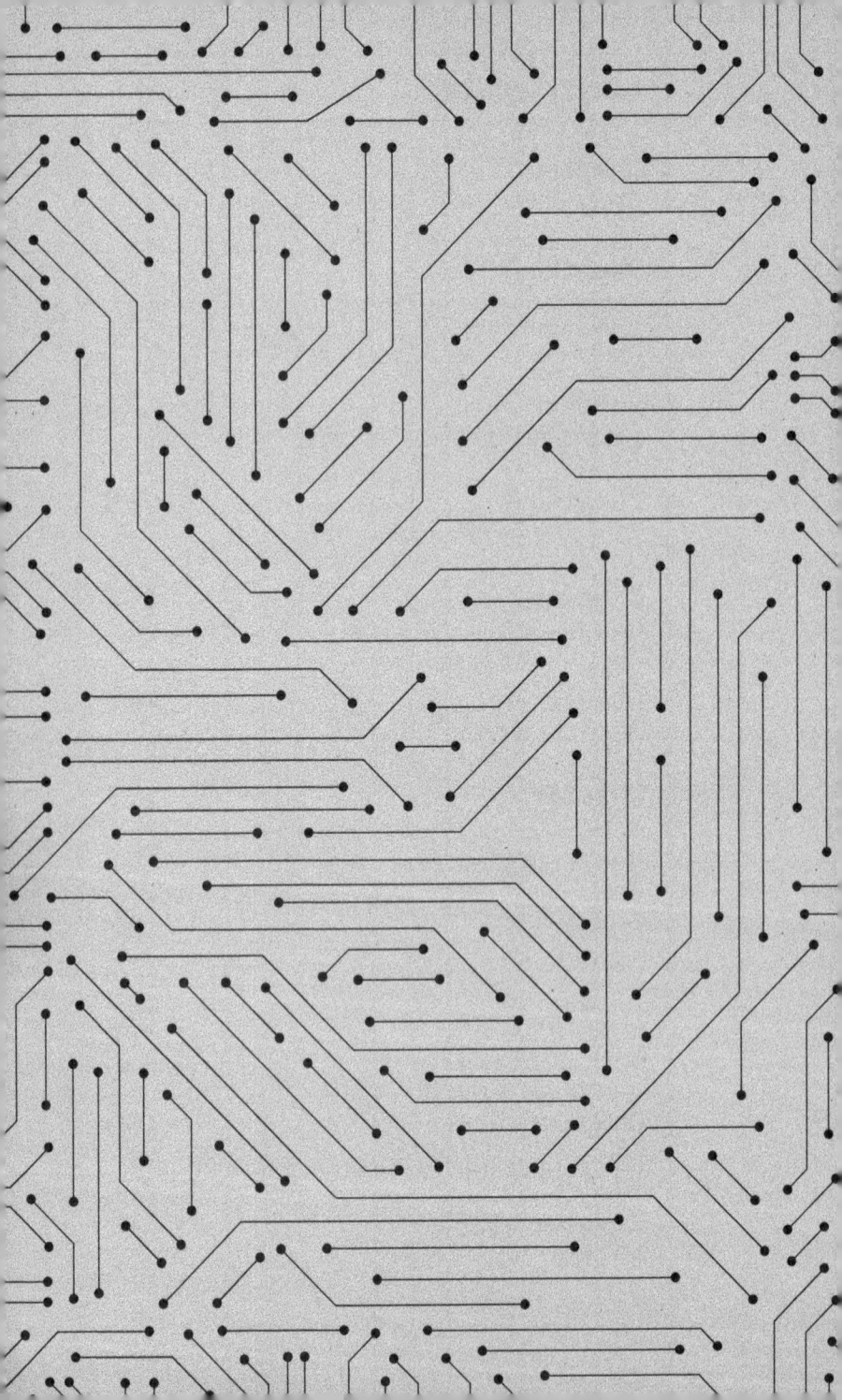

CHAPTER 1 ◻ ✕

uploading . . .

All your AI questions answered

(Oh, and we'll also program a cool
new video game called *Space Pilot*!)

ok

I don't know about you, but it seems
that everyone is talking about AI. It's
everywhere, transforming our lives,
worrying your parents and maybe
even writing your homework (**though
it shouldn't be – and you'll discover
more about why later!**).

But when we say **'artificial intelligence'** or 'AI', what do you imagine? What images pop up in your head? A plastic brain floating in a giant test tube, maybe glowing neon green? How about a giant scary robot coming at you menacingly? Or a massive computer humming away in an empty room with blinking red lights?

That's the funny thing about artificial intelligence – everyone is talking about it, but most people don't know what it is. I mean for real, in the real world, doing real things. They may have seen it in a movie or a video game. They've certainly heard people talking about it on TV, online or at work and school.

BUT WHAT IS ARTIFICIAL INTELLIGENCE REALLY?

Well, that's what we are going to explore in this book. First, we're going to define AI and talk about all the hidden – and not so hidden – places that it's being used today. Then we're going to talk about the future of AI. Or, more importantly, how AI might help you create your future. Maybe you want to become a marine biologist? AI is changing the way we study oceans. Professional footballer? AI's impact on sports will prove even bigger than winning the World Cup (OK, that's a lie, but its impact will be huge!).

Want to become a doctor or veterinarian? You won't believe how much AI is teaching us about animals of every kind.

Sure, there's scary stuff out there (cue the menacing robots). We'll cover that too, mostly to show how the sinister side of AI isn't all it's cracked up to be.

And as with most things in life:

There are things you can do today that will help you prepare for tomorrow.

I'm here to help you do just that! My name is **Brian David Johnson** (most people call me BDJ) and I'm a futurist – which is as cool as it sounds. I help governments, universities, businesses of all types and regular people just like you look into the future and understand what it will be like to live there. I don't make predictions; you won't find a single crystal ball in my office. Instead, I offer people a range of possible futures based on my research. These are things that **COULD** happen or things that **MIGHT** happen. I explore and show people the realm of possible futures so that when the future arrives, they'll be ready for it instead of worrying about it.

Every day, I help people and organisations create the future they want by thinking a few steps ahead, then working backwards to come up with a plan that will take them there. It's the same thing with AI. You can get stressed out imagining a bunch of scary scenarios. Or you can grasp what the technology is and where it's going and then make it your friend in helping you imagine, and then realise, the future of your dreams. That's why I wrote this book.

Along the way, I'm going to introduce you to a bunch of new ideas, as well as some of the people who know the most about AI, **because they're the ones who are actively building it today.**

Oh, one more thing! In addition to being a futurist, I love coming up with fun ways to talk about science and technology – I'm a huge fan of sci-fi movies and graphic novels, and I've even written a bunch of action–adventure books. **So I promise to make this one a lot of fun, too!**

WHAT IS AI?

Right, then, enough with the introductions. Let's get on with it.

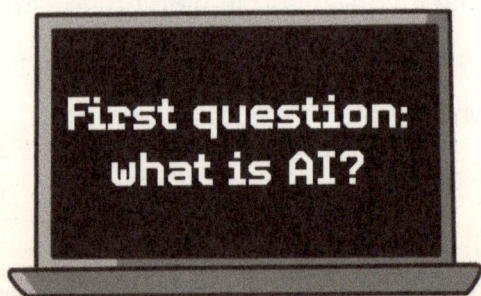

First question: what is AI?

The term artificial intelligence was coined in 1956 by a computer scientist named John McCarthy. He was at a conference at Dartmouth University in New Hampshire, USA with a bunch of academics who were devising new ways for computers to perform advanced tasks, along the lines of the human brain.

But at its core, AI is nothing more than a **new kind of software that runs on a computer.**

That's it.

I know what you're thinking: wait, there's got to be more to it than that! And sure, it gets a little more complicated. But as we continue this journey, I want you to never lose sight of the fact that **AI is just *software*.**

Don't believe me? Let's ask an expert . . .

ASK THE EXPERT:

Reid Blackman,
philosopher, professor and ethicist

Reid Blackman helps governments and companies figure out how to best use AI. He often has to explain what AI is, in the easiest way possible, to a whole lot of people. He says:

The best way to describe AI is that it's software that learns by example. You do that all the time. If I give you a bunch of examples (like photos) of what gorvatzs look like, I bet you'll be able to point out the gorvatz if I give you a new picture. (And no, there's no such thing as a gorvatz. I made that up.)

Let's say you want the AI to recognise Gerald, your corgi. You would give the software pictures of Gerald and tell the software, 'This is Gerald the corgi.' Just like you, the software will learn what Gerald looks like and can then point him out in new pictures.

By the way, if you want a fancy word for 'example' you can use the word 'data'. So AI is software that learns from data. The software analyses the data of the pictures of Gerald and it learns what the data looks like in those photos. It finds 'the Gerald pattern' in the data. Once it knows the Gerald pattern, it can look for it in new photos. When it finds the Gerald pattern, it says, 'Yup, that's Gerald!'

That's it. AI is software that learns by data.

So if AI is just software, why is it so hard for people to understand? Part of the problem is it got stuck with a seriously unfortunate name.

Let's face it, **'artificial'** and **'intelligence'** are a strange mix of words. It's almost an oxymoron (the fancy term for when opposite words are thrown together). Imagine phrases like 'living dead' or 'deafening silence' or another of my favourites from the early years of computers, 'virtual reality'.

How about we split the phrase 'artificial intelligence' in two and look at each word separately?

artificial   intelligence

Artificial:

◪ ✕

This adjective usually refers to something bad. If a person is artificial, we don't want to be around them. Artificial is fake. It's not real. Things like artificial flowers are not nearly as nice to give to your mum as fresh flowers. Every grown-up will tell you not to eat artificial foods. The chemicals in them aren't good for you. And no one would choose to stretch out and nap on artificial grass if they could find a nice soft patch of natural grass instead.

✕

So the word artificial is often **BAD**.

Intelligence:

◪ ✕

The other half of AI is very much a good thing. If a person is called intelligent, they are smart and likely to be successful in life. There are astronauts and scientists who search the universe for intelligent life. People like dogs because they are intelligent – they listen to their owners. They're trainable and they can even do tricks!

✕

So the word intelligence is often **GOOD**.

Well, of course these words are confusing when you put them together. They're opposing ideas that bring up totally different values. And yet we use them to describe an **amazing technology** that can do incredible things that will make all our lives better. It's no wonder people don't understand it.

A BRIEF HISTORY OF THE COMPUTER, THE INTERNET AND BEYOND . . .

Since we're going to talk a lot about software in this book, it's important to understand the computer. You're probably thinking to yourself, *Come on, BDJ, I know what a computer is!* I get it. But computers aren't just the things you use to write essays or surf the internet. Computers today are found in all kinds of electronic devices, from cars to washing machines.

How did that happen?

The history of the computer is fascinating and filled with a lot of amazing people who made the computers we have today possible. But here's a **VERY** quick tour. Hold on to your hats . . .

Computers are all about mathematics, which goes back thousands of years. But in the interest of time, let's skip ahead several millennia to the early 1800s, when an Englishman named **Charles Babbage** invented the first mechanical computer. Called the **Difference Engine**, it looked nothing like today's computers. But it was the first programmable computer to crunch numbers on its own, so a lot of people call Babbage the **'Father of Computers'**.

Working with Babbage was **Ada Lovelace**. She is credited as the first person to write a computer program or algorithm to be run on one of Babbage's computers, making her the **'First Computer Programmer'**!

The next giant leap forward came in 1936, when another Englishman called **Alan Turing** devised something called the a-machine (short for 'automated machine'). It was more of an idea than a physical object – one in which machines were able to solve all kinds of incredibly complex problems. **The Turing Machine**, as it came to be known, changed the world by revealing just how far computers could take us.

Early computers were controlled by machine code, which uses ones and zeros to tell the computer what to do. Machine code is difficult to learn, so we needed a better way for people to program computers. In the 1950s, an American computer scientist called **Grace Hopper** pioneered a new way to write programs using English words rather than just ones and zeros. These types of programming languages are called high-level languages, and they made writing programs for computers much easier, so more people could be trained to do it. Hopper's work was used to create the programming language called **COBOL**, which stands for 'common business-oriented language'.

The software language she helped create way back then is still used today.

Fast forward another twenty-five years. Computer scientists all over the world had been tinkering with the concept of the computer, and companies like **IBM had developed the first personal computer** (PC). Though the earliest PCs were often big enough to take up an entire room. Not very personal!

That all changed in 1976, when a couple of college dropouts named **Steve Jobs** and **Steve Wozniak** started a company called **Apple**. In the same year, working out of Jobs' garage in Los Altos, California, the dynamic duo launched the Apple computer. The first Apple computer was small enough and user-friendly enough for people to bring into their homes. Apple sales jumped from $7.8 million in 1978 to $117 million in 1980. **It was game on for the computer!**

We use the internet every day. But it had to be invented too, by some very big minds in the field of computer science. In 1984, one of the brainiest of the brunch, a network engineer named **Radia Perlman**, developed a standardised way for computers to communicate with each other on a network. It worked so well that other programmers started to use it, making Perlman the **'Mother of the Internet'**. I was fortunate to work with Radia when I worked at a big company in America called the Intel Corporation!

In the decades since, computers have become smaller and faster and more powerful. In the process, they have found their way into phones, tellies, watches, cars, appliances, planes – you name it. If it runs on electronics, chances are it uses a computer.

TAKING A HARD LOOK AT SOFTWARE

It's too late to come up with a better name for AI. But we can still think about the technology more clearly. As I've said a few times now, AI is just software. Even that term is a bit of a head scratcher, since software isn't something you can touch and feel, like a soft blanket. The more accurate name might be invisi-ware. Doesn't have the same ring to it, I know – so software it is!

OK, so now we have a better understanding of computers and how they're used in everything around us, let's look a little deeper . . .

Hardware and software are a computer's two main components.

Hardware: ◩ ☒

This is the name for the physical pieces of a computer that you can touch and feel. In the case of a laptop, it's the keyboard you type on and the monitor you look at. With a phone, it's the buttons you press and the speaker that sound comes out of. Hardware is also all the circuits and microchips and such that are hidden away inside any computer. You can't see this hardware, but it's there.

Software: ◩ ☒

If we think of hardware as the body of the computer, software is the brains. It's the programs and applications that run on a computer. Because software is based on digital information, it can't be seen and handled the way hardware can (invisi-ware, I tell you!). On a computer, software is the program you use to write an essay or design a presentation. On a phone, it's the app you open to order takeaway.

So let's ask the question again:

If AI is just software, what's the big deal?

Why are so many people talking about it? Why are some people even frightened of it?

To answer those questions, we need to talk more about how software is made – or more specifically, how software is written. Writing software programs lets us do things like calculate numbers, make apps for our phones and even play video games.

Hmmm . . . video games. That's it! Let's use video games to show the difference between standard computer software and software that's been supercharged by AI.

Yes, AI is just software. But it's not just any old software, like the kind used to call up a webpage on the internet or find the best route on your phone's GPS. AI software is **supercharged**. To show you what I mean, let's imagine you decide to make a video game called *Space Pilot*. The goal of the game is to steer a tricked-out spaceship around a distant alien planet that is light years away from Earth.

The pilot is all alone and they need to navigate their research mission across an alien planet to map its surface. But to do this they must avoid crashing into the planet's scary mountain monsters. Sounds good, yes?

To program *Space Pilot*, you need to code the software so that when the player presses left on their game controller, their spaceship on the screen will move left. Then you need to write some more code that tells the software that when the player presses right on the game controller, the spaceship will move right on the screen and the same for up and down.

You get the idea. When you program a piece of software, you are telling the video game how to react when a player makes an action on their controller. I know this is super simple, but stick with me, because it's about to get a lot more interesting!

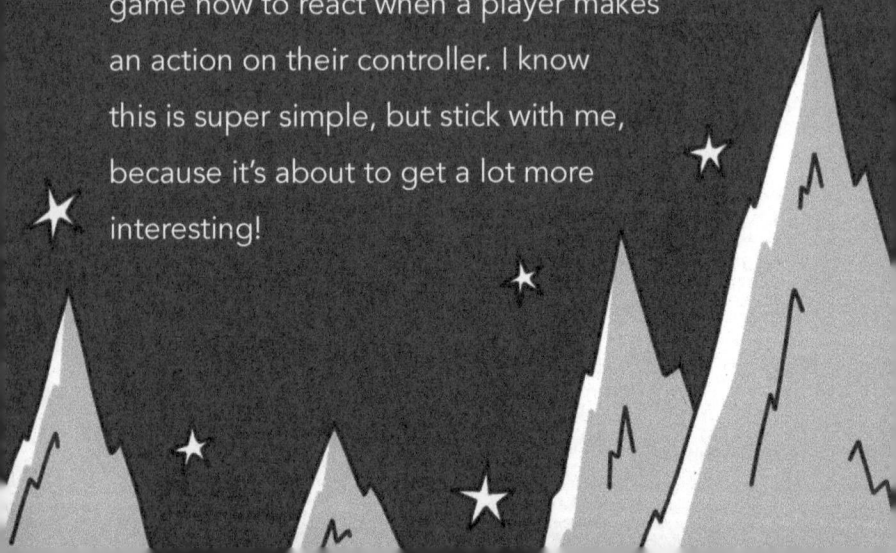

Coding uncoded

People who develop software are called programmers or software developers, and the technique they use is called coding or programming. In the simplest terms, code or a program is a set of instructions that a computer follows to complete a given task. A good way to think of coding is like cooking. Cooks follow a recipe to create a dish. Computers follow coding to create a program. The **'recipe'** of coding is based on a series of numerical or alphabetical sequences. The simplest form, binary code, consists solely of zeros and ones. It can be difficult to learn. High-level code is designed to be easier to understand than binary code and this makes it easier to write much more complicated sequences of instructions known as algorithms. Complicated algorithms are used to create AI.

In the future we will use AI to write code for us, which we would then refine or adapt to suit our purpose. **A software that writes software!**

Now let's imagine your *Space Pilot* video game on AI. Let's call this 2.0 version *Space Pilot 2 – Alien Planet Revenge!!!* It's still the same basic concept, with an intrepid space traveller navigating an alien universe far, far away. But there is *a lot* more going on around the player in this version of the game. The reason for this lies in a single word – **complexity**.

I'm sure you're familiar with the word complex. It's the opposite of simple, right? Meaning there are more moving parts or concepts to process and understand. In computer science, complexity refers to things like the total number of steps and the amount of memory a computer needs to carry out each piece of code. And as we know, code is the building block used to develop a piece of software.

Your second edition of *Space Pilot* involves a level of complexity that is *much* more sophisticated. In the first edition, you allowed the player to **move left, right, up and down to avoid the treacherous mountains on the surface of the alien planet**. In the new and improved version, your pilot has been transported to a different alien planet. And this one is far worse than the first.

In your new game there are **not only more complex mountains** on the surface of the planet, coming from below to destroy the ship – there are also *cloud mountains* coming from above.

But we don't stop there!

The surface mountains (the ones coming from below the ship) are so tall that they also have **new mountains sprouting, growing and**

shooting from their sides. That means mountains are coming at the space pilot from the **left and the right** as well.

Basically, there are scary dangerous mountain monsters everywhere! In fact, there are so many scary dangerous mountain monsters that the player can **no longer see the spaceship on the screen**! Our space pilot is lost inside a maze of mountains.

Here's the question: If the player can't see the ship, how will they successfully navigate the space pilot across the alien planet to map the surface? It's so complex it seems impossible for the player to win the game.

That's where AI comes in.

Imagine if you could program the game to study all the possible pathways the spacecraft could take through the mountains. In this way you are training the software on all the possible routes through the mountains. Some are successful, but more end in doom and the ship crashing. You could tell the software to find the best and safest path through the mountains on its own. The software could then go out and explore every possible pathway and come up with the best one.

In this video game example, the infinite number of pathways through the mountain landscape are called data. Because its programming has complexity, AI-enhanced software can explore them all at the same time. A century ago, a computer was considered fast if it could process a few thousand commands per second.

In the AI age, computers can now handle around **10 trillion**!

With AI at the helm in *Space Pilot*, it can play multiple games and fly the spaceship in every direction through the mountains. By doing this over and over, all inside a split second, the software can collect an enormous amount of data. Then it can use a tool called **probability** to figure out which pathway is the safest.

Probability is how likely something is to happen.

As our AI-enhanced spaceship sorts through 10 trillion mountain passes at once, it uses probability to rule out any that are likely to end up in a fiery crash.

This is what makes AI so powerful. Using complex algorithms, it can explore and get trained on an incredibly complex data set (in this case, pathways through an alien mountain planet) and then determine the route that has the highest probability of success. And it can pull off this amazing feat a trillion times faster than any human.

This might sound superhuman and a little scary, too. But let me assure you that it's not. To make that point more clearly, let's think about our friend the calculator.

AI AND THE CALCULATOR

We all know that a calculator can do maths faster than most humans. But the electronic device isn't considered scary or superhuman, right? It's just a calculator, a tool that helps us do complex sums incredibly fast. **Think of AI like a next-level calculator**, performing complex calculations with massive amounts of data and algorithms. AI can also be trained from the various calculations and make decisions based on its training. In this sense, it's able to **mimic human intelligence** and decision making. This is the key difference between regular software and software that's been given a turbo-boost from AI.

This is also where the fear factor comes in for a lot of people. If computers can process lots of information and make decisions like humans, what's to stop them from getting together and taking over the world?

This question is at the heart of the **fear** surrounding AI.

As an engineer and a futurist, I believe AI is an amazing tool that will continue to improve the world. But I also appreciate that not everyone thinks like me.

Maybe they've watched a lot of science-fiction movies where **AI is a force for evil**. As a sci-fi nerd, I love these stories. They're exciting and fun to watch, but they're not all that factually correct. That's because AI, like all technological advancements, is evolving over time and not all at once. Think how long it took for the first computer to turn into an Apple PC (more than a hundred and fifty years) and then how long again it was until the launch of the first Apple iPhone (another thirty

years). But a movie about how AI is changing the world every day in small ways wouldn't sell a lot of tickets. So, we're left with AI-enhanced robots suddenly rising up against us.

Another big reason people are scared of AI is because they feel like they don't have any control over it. They aren't the ones flying the *Space Pilot* ship any more. The computer is in control. That makes people wonder what else they won't be able to control in the future. After all, if computers can basically process information and make decisions for themselves, then what control will we meagre humans have over the future?

What's to stop machines from getting together and taking over the world?

The answer: we are.

MYTH BUSTER

The Myth: Because AI is a computer, it's always right.

The Truth: Because AI software runs on a computer, it's easy to think of it as a neutral player – one that never chooses sides. But as we continue this journey together, I want you to always remember that **AI is only as good as the data that people feed it**. That means it can be exposed to the same human prejudices and errors that have existed throughout history. For example, some AI software that is being used today by companies to help find new workers can favour certain applicants over others based on old, bad data around race or gender.

The engineers and computer scientists who are developing AI have a saying for this which has been around for many years: 'garbage in = garbage out'.

This is why it's so important for people who work with the technology (and that might include you someday!) to make sure they don't automatically think that the answers they are getting from AI are correct. We always need to interrogate the answers.

Here's an example of outdated prejudices, preconceived notions and bias. Say you asked the AI what sports girls do and don't like to play and it answers, 'Girls like dancing and hate football'. Now, you can use your human brain to know this just isn't true. We know that girls can and do like all different kinds of sports. Unfortunately, whatever data THIS AI was trained on is old and outdated. It was not taught that girls can also like football. It's up to us humans to recognise that error in the data and fix it!

THE FUTURE AND AI

As it turns out, we are not competing against machines. They are not here to take our future from us. Even if they wanted to, they couldn't. **Why?** Because we control the future.

Let me explain. The future is not some fixed point in time that we are all hurtling towards helplessly. **The future is built by people**. This is what my work as a futurist is all about. We as humans imagine our futures, then we go about building them. This has been going on since the beginning of humanity and it will continue until the end of time (which isn't anytime soon, I assure you!). As a futurist, I know that we will imagine and build the future we want – one filled with miraculous breakthroughs. We can also plan and prepare for any possible negative futures or outcomes, to prevent them from happening. This is what this book is all about. You'll absolutely walk away crammed with loads of knowledge about AI and all the cool stuff it's already doing. But you will also be able to start imagining, preparing and building the future that you want, using the **possibilities** of AI.

ONE MORE THING . . .

This book is called *What You Need to Know About AI*. And this book **IS** that. But I must confess something: there are always going to be new things that pop up around AI. New innovations, new breakthroughs. There will always be people coming up with fresh ideas for how to use AI. **That's what makes it all so exciting.**

So here's the truth. This book contains **ALMOST** everything you need to know about AI. That's not a bad thing, though, because it means you can be part of the team that keeps on improving AI, especially after reading this book.

BUT . . . in the last chapter, I'm going to tell you the secret for how you can **ALWAYS** know everything you need to know about AI. It's not a trick, I promise. It's a way for you to always be up to date on the latest and greatest. To always know what you need to know about AI.

(You can skip ahead if you like . . . I won't tell!)

Before we get to that, let's take a tour of AI in action, by looking at some of the different and amazing things that AI is doing now and will continue doing in the future. This gets at the **'why'** of the matter.

Why is AI so important?

Why is everyone talking about it?

The answer has to do with the fact that AI is impacting just about every aspect of our lives, in ways that are big and small. We're going to zoom in on some areas where AI is helping us already – from understanding dinosaurs, volcanoes, space and the bottom of the ocean to revolutionising entertainment, medicine, transport and even animal care!

Along the way, we'll also explore the aspects of AI that lots of people are worried about. As we touch on those scarier topics, I want you to remember what this futurist told you earlier in the book: **you don't have to worry about the future**. Why? Because by facing the future **RIGHT HERE** and **RIGHT NOW**, by reading this book, you are preparing yourself today for what's coming tomorrow.

DID YOU KNOW?

Artificial intelligence is also a blanket term that describes a whole bunch of other cool and interesting technologies. Throughout this book, I'll call attention to these other terms in the Quick Tech Take boxes.

But before we embark, let's ask another expert for their advice . . .

ASK THE EXPERT:

Dr Genevieve Bell,
cultural anthropologist, futurist and professor

Dr Genevieve Bell is a cultural anthropologist, futurist, and Distinguished Professor at the Australian National University. I have worked with Genevieve for many years, and I asked her how she thought I could frame the complexity of AI for you. She laughed and replied:

You have to understand that AI isn't just AI.

What I mean by that is that when people talk about AI, they aren't just talking about the AI-enhanced software by itself. It doesn't exist by itself. AI needs a lot of other things to work. It needs massive amounts of data but it also needs a connection to the internet. It needs sensors as a connection to the physical world around us and applications that use all this intelligence to perform tasks for us.

There's a lot . . .

But most importantly, AI needs people. It needs people to program it. To run it. To maintain it and keep it running. It needs people to use it. If a human isn't using AI, does it really matter at all if it's just sitting out there on its own doing stuff?

It's all about the humans. The human impact is what makes AI so massively impressive. Without the humans, AI isn't really important at all.

OK, let's get started . . . .

CHAPTER 2

▱ ✕

uploading . . .

AI and sport:

Dinosaurs, volcanoes and the bottom of the ocean

ok

A VISION OF THE FUTURE . . .

On the Indonesian island of Java, citizens pack up their homes and move many miles away from the active volcano that looms over their city. They do this because they've been warned by scientists that the volcano is going to erupt – in ten days! The early warning is thanks to AI and its ability to predict volcanic activity almost down to the hour. No lives will be lost when the lava in Java starts to flow . . .

Meanwhile, on the other side
of planet Earth, in the ocean off Greenland,
marine biologists discover another lost city,
this one located 8 kilometres underwater!
The discovery will provide fresh insights
into how civilisations evolve . . .

And in a small village in South West England,
a ten-year-old boy takes his pet for a walk.
None of the villagers seems bothered by the
fact that it's a 3.5 metre tall T. rex!

The power of AI is its ability to process massive amounts of information in the **blink of an eye** (actually, even faster than that, but you get the point!). Technological development often involves taking very big things and making them more manageable.

To explain what I mean, let's think about travel, or the act of getting from point A to point B. We'll use the example of travelling 160 kilometres (100 miles). If we go way back in time, the earliest humans needed about 50 hours to cover that distance by foot. When they learned to ride horses, that cut the time in half, to around 25 hours. Then came the bicycle, which lets a typical rider travel 160 kilometres in 15 hours or less. The invention of the automobile dropped the travel time to under 2 hours. A commercial

plane can fly 160 kilometres in about 12 minutes. And a spaceship? Hurtling through the cosmos at an average speed of 28,000 kilometres per hour, it needs only about 0.006 seconds to travel 160 kilometres! If we do the maths, we see that technology has decreased human travel time by approximately 10,000%. Not bad!

It's the same with AI. This turbo-boosted computer software is making it possible to tackle big ideas in ways never thought possible before. In this chapter, we'll look at a few of my favourites.

Now, when I called this chapter 'gigantic things', I meant **GIGANTIC**. Not just 'big'. Big things are of 'considerable size'. Big things are **OK**, but gigantic is better . . . even better than **HUGE**.

Let's start with what are probably the coolest gigantic things out there – **dinosaurs!**

GIGANTIC THINGS THAT GO ROAR!

Dinosaurs were reptiles that roamed the planet a long, long time ago – starting about 250 million years ago, during the Triassic period.

WHAT'S YOUR FAVOURITE DINO?
- Tyrannosaurus rex
- Brachiosaurus
- Triceratops
- Velociraptor
- Titanosaur

My favourite dinos are the little guys and the massive sea creatures. I like the Microraptor, which means **'little thief'** in the Greek language. It was one of the smallest dinos and it had

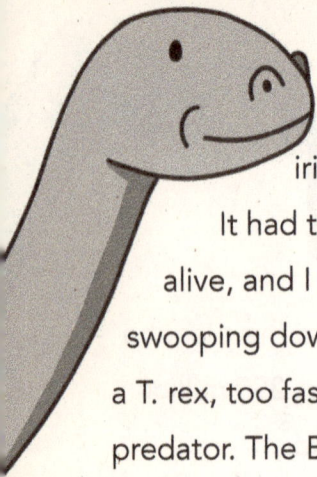

iridescent feathers like a peacock. It had to be really good at staying alive, and I like to imagine the Microraptor swooping down from a tree and flying past a T. rex, too fast to be caught by the massive predator. The Brachiosaurus and the T. rex are big and flashy, but I like the little guys.

I also like the **BIG** guys in the ocean. When I stare out at the ocean, I like to imagine what massive creatures and sea monsters could have swum through those waters. The Shonisaurus sikanniensis is my favourite. Scientists estimate it was 21 metres long – that's almost the size of two double-decker coaches put together!

A LITTLE DINO HISTORY

The dinos' reign on earth came to an end about 65 million years ago, at the end of the Cretaceous period. Thanks to the work of **palaeontologists**, we've come to learn a lot about dinosaurs, mainly by finding and piecing together their fossils or bones and other body parts that have been preserved in sand, mud and other sediment. If you've ever been to a dinosaur exhibit at a museum, you know from these fossil recreations that dinosaurs were **GIGANTIC**. T. rex, for example, could grow to around 12 metres long and 3.5 metres tall!

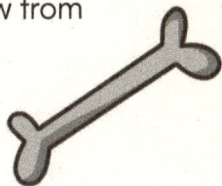

And if you've ever seen the *Jurassic Park* movies, you know that dinosaurs have escaped museums and made their way into the imagination of filmmakers, like Steven Spielberg.

Dinosaur movies are a lot of fun. **But it's important to remember that they're also works of fiction.**

Armed with AI, palaeontologists can start seeing what dinosaurs would have looked like for *real*, how they would have walked, when they lived and much more. And they are using the software to classify and understand dinosaurs more quickly than ever before. Now, when a palaeontologist finds fossils or fragments of a dinosaur, they can use AI software to fit the pieces together and fill in any missing holes. So if they only find a few bones, AI can help them work out what bones they are missing. Or if a team of palaeontologists discover a dinosaur footprint during a dig, they can use AI to figure out which species made it.

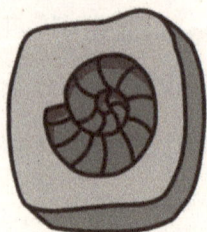

They do this by feeding thousands of different pictures and data points about dinosaurs into a computer. AI-powered software then analyses the data and compares it to the unknown footprint. Within a split second, the system gives the palaeontologists the most probable dinosaur match to the newly discovered footprint.

Breakthroughs in our understanding of the dinosaur planet that used to take years can now happen in minutes! It's all made possible by something called machine learning.

QUICK TECH TAKE:

Machine learning

Machine learning is one of the building blocks of AI. It's the ability of a machine to imitate intelligent human behaviour and perform tasks without you having to tell the computer how to do it. Examples include a computer recognising what's happening in a picture or video, being able to understand and interpret written text or being able to carry out an action in the physical world, like recognising faces or recommending foods to eat and places to visit.

These machines aren't actually 'learning' in the way that you would learn new things. Machines aren't human. In this case, the machines look for patterns in a set of data and then make predictions based on them, so that they can answer a question or take an action.

Let me give you an example:

Let's say you wanted the AI software to be able to look at a picture and tell if there is a cat in the picture or not.

First, you would feed into the software a whole bunch of different pictures of cats. Remember, not all cats look the same. It might be easy for you to understand that an **orange tabby** and a **sleek Siamese** are both different types of cat, but an AI has no idea until we teach it.

How do we do that? We give it a lot of pictures of cats and tell it, **'This is a cat.'**

Next, we show it a lot of other pictures of people and places and things — some of which have cats and some of which don't.

Then we ask the AI to show us all the pictures that have cats.

It will come back and give us all the pictures that include cats. And you know what – it will be *kind* of right. It will get some of the pictures correct, but it will miss a lot of cats.

So then we need to show it more picture of cats so it can **'learn'**. But again, remember, it's **NOT** learning like you learn. It's using the pictures of cats that we are giving it to make a guess, with high probability, that there is a cat in this picture. It doesn't even know what a cat looks like until we refine its **'learning'**.

This is why it's called **machine learning**. The great thing about it is that machines work very fast, so we can **'teach'** the machine about cats very quickly.

It gets even better. With all the newfound knowledge about dinosaurs, palaeontologists can work with computer animators to create cool, lifelike pictures and videos of what dinosaurs really looked like in the real world. Up until now, they've had to rely on **educated guesses** (based on science, yes, but still just guesses). Filmmakers like Steven Spielberg based their own imaginings of the dinosaur planet on these guesses.

But now we're getting a much more accurate understanding of what dinosaurs looked like and how they lived. Machine learning can do things like help palaeontologists identify which dinosaur particular bone fragments or teeth came from, or recognise tiny differences in fossilised dinosaur footprints to tell us how they walked. And in the future, that understanding is going to become **clearer and clearer**. This will enable people like you to create dinosaur worlds based on vast libraries of fossils that have been digitised in museums. You'll even be able to create a pet dinosaur of your own! Though you won't have to worry about it eating your best friend or little brother, because it will only exist as a 3D image. **Phew!**

GIGANTIC THINGS THAT GO BOOM!

Whereas the dino is a really cool gigantic thing, volcanoes can be a little more scary, especially when they erupt. AI has the power to make them less scary by telling us when they're about to go boom.

Scientists who study volcanoes are known as volcanologists. Today, they use a lot of fancy equipment to measure the activity of volcanoes all over the world. That includes

seismographs, which measure
the seismic waves produced by
earthquakes, and a type of spectrometer
which can measure volcanic gases in the air.

All this information has helped volcanologists
get much better at predicting volcanic eruptions.
But as with palaeontologists and dinosaurs, their
predictions are still just educated guesses. With
AI software, these guesses are getting more and
more accurate. That's thanks to something called
PREDICTIVE ANALYTICS.

Remember *Space Pilot* from the last chapter?
AI used **probability** – the likelihood of whether
something would happen or not – to figure out
which pathway across the alien planet was the
safest. Predictive analytics builds on that idea by
using data to predict future events.

QUICK TECH TAKE:

Predictive analytics

Predictive analytics is the use of data and statistical algorithms to figure out the probability of future outcomes based on historical information. Woah! That sounds complex, right? Basically, its goal is to figure out what is most likely to happen in the future based on things that happened in the past. Phew, that's much easier.

How does this work?

It goes back to the data.

Volcanologists gather a whole bunch of readings from the past when volcanoes made noise and did or didn't erupt. There are patterns in that data which show that if a volcano makes one specific sound or vibration, it probably is going to erupt, but if it makes a different sound or vibration, it may not.

The AI, using predictive analytics, doesn't know for **sure** if the volcano is going to blow, but it can make a pretty good **guess** or **prediction** based on the massive amount of data and sounds collected previously.

Volcanologists today are busy feeding decades' worth of data involving seismic activity into AI software programs. These programs can sift through all this data and compare information about volcanoes all over the world. The computer is basically listening to the Earth's rumblings to know what they sounded like one month, one week, one day and one second before a specific volcano erupted. The computer is also distinguishing between different rumbles.

DID YOU KNOW?

Every volcano makes a unique sound. Volcanoes in Alaska have different rumblings to volcanoes in South America. In fact, just like every person has a unique voice, every volcano has its own rumble!

Volcanologists are not there yet, but AI will enable a future where they can predict with 99.9% accuracy when each of the Earth's approximately 1,500 active volcanoes are getting ready to blow (unfortunately, there's no such thing as 100% accuracy, even with help from AI). This will serve as an early warning system for people living near volcanoes and help make our world a safer place.

ONE OF THE MOST GIGANTIC THINGS ON EARTH!

Now, there is something even more gigantic than a dino or a volcano: the ocean. Some 71% of the Earth's surface is covered by ocean. That means there is more land underwater than above it, where you and I live. What's more, only about a fifth of the land underwater has been mapped by humans. We don't know what the rest of it looks like and we certainly don't know what lives down there. Most people know more about our solar system than they do about the bottom of our own oceans!

People who study oceans are called oceanographers. Like volcanologists, they use sophisticated equipment to do their jobs. Satellite-based altimeters are devices that measure the shape (known as the topography) of land beneath the water. Sonar, on the other hand, detects the distance and direction of objects under the water, by analysing sound waves coming off rock formations and deep-sea creatures. **And here's the coolest bit of equipment you've all been waiting for...**

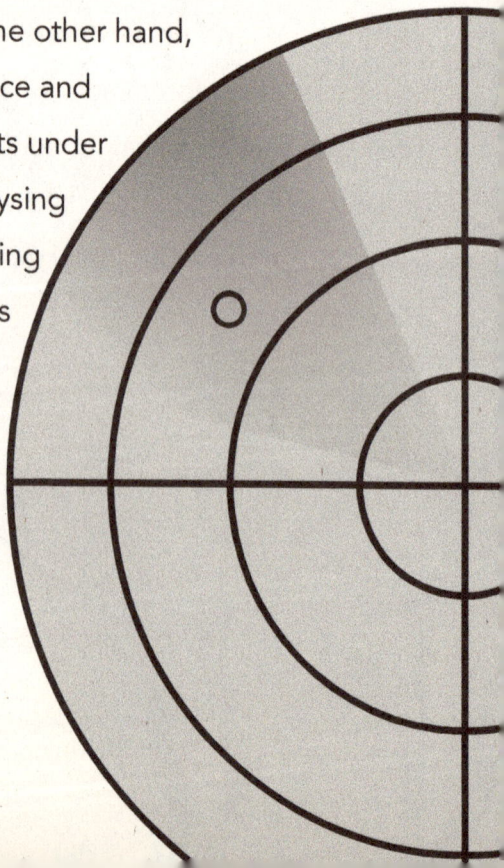

UNDERWATER ROBOTS!

(Don't worry, we will get deeper into ALL robots in a later chapter.)

UUVs (short for **'unmanned underwater vehicles'**) can perform all sorts of tasks, like collecting seafloor samples and exploring old shipwrecks. They are important to oceanographers because it's dangerous for humans to travel too far underwater. And the ocean is *deep*.

The Mariana Trench, located between Guam and the Philippines, is the deepest point known on Earth, at over 10,900 metres below sea level.

That's almost 11 kilometres down – or nearly 30 Empire State Buildings stacked end to end.

No human could survive down there. But an AI-enhanced robot won't mind the assignment. Just like our *Space Pilot* video game, **UUVs** that are powered by AI can make the journey to the bottom of the ocean and collect all kinds of data. And because they're machines, they can stay underwater for a long time. They don't need to come up for air or food. The data can then be fed into computers that generate accurate models of the ocean.

Unlocking the mysteries of the ocean will have so many benefits for humanity. For example, oceanographers will be able to better track internal waves (those happening beneath the surface), which will help in the tapping of hydropower. That's where the **energy in moving water is harnessed and turned into power** for homes, offices, cars and anything else that runs on electricity.

An accurately modelled ocean will also make it easier for **climate scientists** to monitor sea ice. This will provide a much clearer picture of the effects of climate change, as well as efforts to contain it.

Marine biologists, meanwhile, will use AI to keep tabs on the ten thousand known species of algae that are floating through the ocean. They can use the **UUVs** to gather samples to monitor the health and activity of the algae. This will help them reduce damage to the environment, while promoting human health.

The ocean, like volcanoes and dinosaurs, is gigantic. Though scientists have made huge strides in understanding it, it has always been too big to fully understand. AI has the power to change that. For the first time ever, we're beginning to understand what the Earth really looked like when dinosaurs roamed it. We're starting to understand how we can predict when a volcano will erupt. And we're finally getting an accurate picture of the bottom of the ocean.

These discoveries are having **GIGANTIC** benefits not just for humans, but for all species.

CHAPTER 3

■ ✕

uploading . . .

AI and sport:
Putting YOU in the game

ok

A VISION OF THE FUTURE . . .

In a small town two hours west of Lagos, Nigeria, a young footballer called Ibrahim is about to have his life changed forever. An AI scout spotted the athlete when his coach uploaded a video of the hometown team's last game. A representative from Manchester United's Youth Academy has just landed in Lagos and is making the trip to see Ibrahim and his family to offer him a scholarship.

Without the AI scout, Ibrahim would have never been discovered by the club.

Years later, when Ibrahim is playing in the Premier League with Manchester United, his parents can't make his first game. Not to worry – with their AI-enabled headsets, they feel like they are in the stands, surrounded by the chanting crowds. Just before the game, Ibrahim pops into their display to thank his parents for all their support.

What's your favourite sport? Football? Formula One? Swimming? Maybe you don't like sport. That's OK too. Though after you read this section, I'll bet you might like sport a little more. That's because AI is changing sport in some really cool ways.

What is the most awesome sporting achievement you've ever seen? A football goal scored from forty yards out? A spectacular hole in one in golf? An impossible 'get' in tennis?

What do all these incredible things have in common? They were performed and pulled off by humans, by **PEOPLE**! It wasn't a robot or technology. It was people. It might have been a professional athlete or your best friend from school, but it's always people. When you get right down to it, sport is all about showing how amazing human beings are.

Sport and athletes of the future are going to be transformed by the effects of AI, but human skill and talent will always be at the heart of it. Here, Ryan Hogan, a futurist who specialises in studying the future of sport, explains . . .

Ryan Hogan,
futurist

First off, I need to say that AI will not replace what coaches do today. Coaches are really important, and all athletes need a human coach to talk to. But in the future, AI will help athletes train and compete better. It will also help keep them healthy.

In the future, AI will put you in the game. You could be an athlete or a fan – regardless of who you are, it will put you in the middle of the game. When I say that, I do mean it literally. I'm excited about AI scouts looking for new and promising talent. A young player who, because of where they live or play, might not have gotten the opportunity to play could be scouted by AI. There are only so many places that a human scout can go, but an AI can watch videos and check stats all over the world.

If you are a young athlete, you will have so many more opportunities to shine with AI helping you.

AI SCOUTS AND ASSISTANT COACHES

As Ryan says, AI will not replace what coaches do already. But it will be one great assistant coach. Today, by analysing an athlete's stats and injury history, AI software can bring to the coach's attention certain skills and attributes for promising new players. In the future, the AI scout might search the world, watching videos and monitoring stats of many different teams at all levels. The AI could understand the existing strengths and weaknesses of a team and search out new players to fill specific skill gaps.

During practice and the game, the AI assistant coach might make suggestions to the coach and team staff for possible strategies. It could also **analyse the opposing team's stats** to find a weakness and make suggestions for a wide range of plays and substitutions.

It's sort of like our *Space Pilot* video game, where AI was able to determine the safest path through the mountainous terrain. In sport, data analysis will help teams compete against opponents who, on paper at least, are far stronger.

QUICK TECH TAKE:
Computer vision technology

Computer vision technology is an area of AI that enables computers to identify and process objects and people in images and videos. It attempts to perform and automate tasks that replicate human capabilities, only faster and more accurately.

BETTER TRAINING

AI is already improving player performance. For example, wearable sensor technology allows trainers and coaches to track athletes during a game or match. In football, they can see how much ground a player covered, how many times they touched the ball and how hard they shot it. In track and field, runners can track the length of their stride, how much they bounce up and down with each step and even how much oxygen they're taking in with each breath. Athletes are always getting more amazing. With AI, the rate of improvement is getting faster and faster. It might even be enough for someone to break the record and run a 3-minute mile. A lot of sport experts think that's physically impossible. But that's what they said about the 4-minute mile. **With AI, all bets are off!**

THE AI SPORTS REPORTER

On any given day, there are millions of sports competitions happening all over the world. Only a tiny fraction of them get covered in the news, whether online, in a newspaper or on the telly. And it's usually just the popular pro teams. What if you want to read about your favourite amateur club? Or about your school's badminton team? Fat chance finding a local sports reporter to cover those contests. In the future, though, AI could answer the call with the use of **natural language processing**. This technology programs computers to receive data and turn it into plain English. In the case of sport, all the stats and data from a competition could be fed into a computer program, which would turn it into a proper match report. So you'd always be able to keep up with your team!

Now, don't get me wrong, there will always be a need for human journalists and writers to provide their unique point of view, personality and expert commentary on a game. But they can't be everywhere all at once.

This is an example of AI-generated content – these could be articles, blogs, images and even movies that are created by AI and then shared across the internet. While there's plenty of excitement around this technology, it's also stirring up a lot of controversy, since sometimes it's hard to tell if an article was written by an AI or a human. AI-generated content can be a source of misinformation if it's not fact checked by a human. In the example of AI-generated sports recaps, what's to prevent the wrong score from being shared? Right now, AI tools are being developed to fact check content and flag misinformation. But it will also be up to the next generation of AI thinkers and experts to carry on this work. I'm confident that will happen. How? Because that's been the story of technology from the beginning – it has always been used by humans to make life better, one small improvement at a time.

QUICK TECH TAKE:
Natural language processing

Natural language processing, or NLP for short, is a branch of AI that gives computers the ability to understand text and spoken words. This allows computers to understand what we are saying when we talk. Think about all the different voices of your family and friends. Then go bigger and think about all the different languages that people speak, and accents that they speak with, all over the world. It's complicated.

NLP takes many different recordings of people talking and allows the computer to start to get an understanding of what they are saying. It is translating what we say out loud to text and code so that the computer can understand. This is like when you talk to your phone and it turns what you say into text. That is NLP today. AI in your phone!

But now imagine what other things NLP could do in the future. As the algorithms that power NLP get more sophisticated, computers will get better and better at figuring out exactly what we're asking them. Someday, they might even be able to read the emotion in our faces and voices.

CATCHING INJURIES BEFORE THEY HAPPEN

If you're a fan of sport, chances are you've watched your favourite player go out with an injury on more than one occasion. It's part of the game. But does it have to be that way? While AI won't be able to eliminate all injuries in sport, it will greatly reduce the chance of injuries happening. That's why sport trainers are so interested in the technology. For one thing, it can help them create personalised diet and training plans based on a player's specific needs. Training staff can also use AI-enhanced computer vision to monitor an athlete and spot an injury before it happens. Maybe it will pick up on the slightest change in a runner's stride, indicating the beginning of a muscle strain. Or a tweak to the angle of delivery of a bowler in cricket, indicating that something is off with their body.

TRAINERS DESIGNED FOR YOU: BETTER SPORT EQUIPMENT

AI is being used today to make better sport equipment too. From trainers to golf clubs to tennis rackets, designers are using AI to develop better, more powerful designs. These advances are allowing athletes to run faster, jump higher and hit balls harder and farther than ever before.

How do they do it?

Let's talk about trainers. Today, AI software can help a designer to analyse the performance of a trainer when used on the pitch, track or court. This is usually done by observing professional athletes, capturing videos of them and feeding these into the software. In this way, the designer, with the help of AI, can keep making the trainer better and better over time. Some designers are even using AI to come up with crazy trainer designs that no one has ever thought of before.

But in the future, it won't just be professional athletes who are being analysed for the best trainer. You might be able to collect your own data and work with an AI to design your own trainer. This could help you optimise your performance, or you might just want the flashiest trainers to wear to school. It will be up to you.

THE BEST FAN EXPERIENCE **EVER!**

If you are a fan of a sport or a team, then you know you can't get enough information about them. You want to know it all – the next big player, who is injured, who is top of their game. Today, you can find out stats and data and you can watch video feeds of the game or match. **But that's nothing ...**

In the future, AI could put you in the middle of the action. Imagine if you could be right down on the pitch in the middle of the action or zooming around the court watching a match from your own personal perspective. The AI could create the images of the players in real time so it would feel like you were in the stands even if you couldn't make it to the stadium. Or what if you could overlay a picture of yourself on your favourite player so that you could see yourself in the game, as if you're playing the game too!

In the future there will be so many ways for you to interact that it will be the best fan experience ever.

The great thing about sport is that it's driven by data and stats, and as we know, AI loves data and stats. This means that AI will help people to become better athletes, while also making the experience of being a fan even more awesome. But remember, it's human talent that will always be at the heart of sport. AI will just help us get better, break more records and achieve ever greater things.

CHAPTER 4 ▣ ☒

uploading . . .

Furry friends and wild animals

[ok]

A VISION OF THE FUTURE . . .

On a sheep farm in Ireland, hundreds of miles from the nearest veterinarian hospital, the farmer notices that one of his sheep is limping badly. He films the animal with his phone and sends it to his computer AI assistant. Seconds later, the computer responds with a diagnosis for what is causing the animal's discomfort . . . Over in the USA, a vet at a clinic in Oregon gets ready for her day by turning on her video monitor.

Her first patient appears on the screen: a six-month-old corgi with a frisky disposition who has been unusually quiet of late. Using a mixture of connected devices in her patients' homes and her AI assistant to analyse the video, audio and diagnostic data she will treat more than fifty animals over the course of the day, without any of them (or their owners) having to set foot in the clinic!

What's your favourite animal? Is it a pet that you have or want to have? Dog? Cat? Hamster? Fish? Or is it a wild animal? Like a lion or elephant or hedgehog?

We've already seen the many ways in which AI is making life better for humans – protecting us from erupting volcanoes and helping us run faster and jump higher, without pulling a muscle in the process. **Surely it can do things to help other animals, too?**

To answer that question, we should start with the data. **Are you starting to see the trend here?** AI's impact on the world almost always starts with data. And as we saw with dinosaurs and oceans and sport, the key is compiling massive amounts of data and then letting the computer work its magic. Like with the alien mountains in our *Space Pilot* video game.

So, what line of work involves a lot of data and information related to pets and animals? What are the professionals who use this data called? **Veterinarians!**

Veterinarians (aka vets) are medical professionals who care for the health of animals, the same way doctors care for people. They use different medical equipment, from surgical tools to X-ray machines, to treat the injuries and illnesses of pets and other animals. Most vets work in a hospital or private clinic, though some travel to farms, ranches or other remote locations.

Vets deal with a lot of information about how to keep animals healthy.

One of the hardest parts of their work is figuring out why an animal is sick. This would be a whole lot easier if pets could talk and just tell them what's wrong (and no, parrots don't count). Alas, AI doesn't have the power to give voice to animals. **Not yet, anyway!**

But AI can serve as the veterinarian's assistant in many cool ways. It is already doing this by zooming through loads of textbooks and articles that exist online about every kind of animal. **Think of it like the most epic crash course in animal care!**

In the future, AI will be able to scan past diagnoses (that's basically the word for what's wrong with an animal when it's sick) from veterinarian clinics and hospitals all over the world. **Imagine that!** Hundreds, thousands, even millions of bits of information about other dogs and cats that might not have been feeling well. And it will be used to help your vet make your pet feel better.

How, exactly? Well, this vast database of information about animals would be stored on a server that any vet can access anytime. They wouldn't even need to type questions into the computer. They could just speak them out loud, the way they do with a human assistant. Using natural language processing, the AI assistant will be able to answer in plain English (or French or Japanese or whatever language the vet happens to speak).

Here's what the exchange might sound like:

> Vet: AI, I have a three-year-old Border Collie with lame hindquarters and swollen lymph nodes. Her weight is also down about 6 kilos. What is the most likely cause?

> AI: Based on my analysis of 3,642 Border Collies in the last twelve months with similar symptoms, the most likely condition is Lyme disease.

Once the vet runs blood tests to confirm the diagnosis, he or she can then ask the AI assistant which course of treatment has been the most effective against the current form of Lyme disease.

Computer vision technology will also come into play with animal care. Vets will take pictures and videos of an animal and load them into the AI computer software. Imagine your cat or rabbit has an unusual skin rash or infected cut. The computer will be able to identify it instantly and suggest the best treatment. Or if a cow or horse is walking oddly, it will pinpoint the joint problem or muscle strain.

As we saw with human athletes, AI might even be able to anticipate health problems with animals **before they happen** and prescribe the best preventative treatment. It could be a thinning in the animal's coat or slight weight loss or even bad breath! All these tiny clues that the vet might miss, even with their years of training and expertise, could be picked up by the AI and used to protect the long-term health of the animal.

It won't stop there, though.

Imagine a world where your pet doesn't have to visit the vet's office at all. I know a lot of dogs and cats who would be **VERY** happy about that.

The same AI assistant might be able to make virtual house calls via your computer or phone, then report back to the vet with a diagnosis and specific steps that will make your pet better.

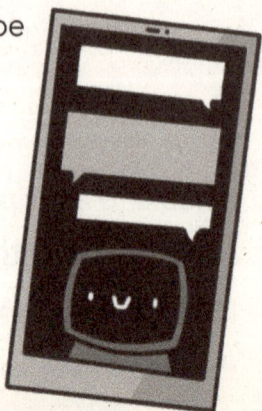

The vet will check the diagnosis and treatment, and work with you to make sure your pet gets the care it needs.

This technology could also be used by animal trainers. Imagine having your own AI dog trainer (I'm not sure about virtual trainers for cats, but maybe . . .). Using the same computer vision technology and natural language processing, the AI assistant would be able to help teach your dog tricks. The human dog trainer would still be the one doing the actual training, but AI could give them all kinds of useful recommendations by interpreting the animal's actions and behaviours, almost like reading their thoughts. It might even be able to analyse and correct bad behaviour, like chewing on your mum's slippers or barking at every car that drives past. That's going to make for a lot more happy pet owners the world over!

ASK THE EXPERT:

Dr Meghan Hook,
veterinarian

Dr Meghan Hook is not just a practising veterinarian. She's my vet! She's been taking care of my furry friends for years. I thought it would be interesting to hear what an actual expert vet thought about their future with AI.

I'm excited about using AI to make my patients healthier.

As you know, pets are bad at telling us what's wrong. The AI diagnostics will really help with that. Things like reading X-rays or scans really quickly and calling out if the AI sees anything wrong. It will allow us to provide care faster and get your pet feeling better more quickly. I'm also excited about using it for remote and in-home care when people and their pets can't make it to my office.

AI won't replace vets. I see it as another tool like my stethoscope. Pets and their owners need to talk with a human. So much of the care of a pet is also taking care of the owner, making sure they understand the diagnosis and treatment. But I'm all for using AI as a tool. If it makes pets and their owners healthier and happier, I think it's great.

INTO THE WILD

What about wild animals? We can't forget them. Just like your pet's vet, vets who care for animals in the wild will benefit from AI.

Remember how oceanographers and marine biologists use AI to track the health of microscopic algae at the bottom of the ocean? Vets will be able to do the same with land creatures, for example, using drones and GPS technology and AI-powered software to monitor endangered animals like elephants and rhinos. They'll track the animals' individual movements to make sure that they're healthy and have access to enough food and water. The AI will **recognise** each animal, analyse the data to understand its current health and co-ordinate the drones to get a close-up image if it's needed. Maybe most importantly, when the drones capture a video of a human, the AI could recognise if it's a game warden there to help or a poacher who might want to hurt the animals.

WHAT IF YOU COULD TALK TO ANIMALS?

I know I said earlier that AI can't teach animals to talk. But that doesn't mean we can't use AI to communicate with them more clearly. Microphones and other forms of advanced sensor technology will allow vets to listen to animals 24/7, which no human could ever do on their own. This will provide **valuable insights** into animal behaviour. For example, listening to the clicks and whistles that whales produce can tell us when they're under stress. It's the same with the roar of a lion, a bird's chirping or any of the millions of unique sounds that are coming out of the animal kingdom.

Animals are communicating with each other all the time. Experts have been able to come up with some idea of what they're saying. But there are too many sounds for them to get a full picture. AI is changing that by analysing the massive amount of data and information in real time to spot patterns of behaviour and make sense of the animal world. One day, the technology might even allow us to not only listen to animals and know what they're saying, but also talk back to them using the recorded and captured sounds!

DID YOU KNOW?

Bats have names. They make individual sounds and can identify each other!

Thanks to AI, not only will we be able to offer better care for our furry friends, but you might even finally be able to know what your dog or cat is thinking and feeling. That will make your bond with your best friend even closer!

CHAPTER 5

▨ ☒

uploading . . .

An extraordinary you

ok

A VISION
OF THE FUTURE . . .

The music ends as Philip finishes his dance routine in front of the mirror. He's out of breath. It's a difficult routine and he's been practising hard. 'How was that?' he asks.

'Much better,' his AI dance coach replies cheerily. With cameras, sensors and AI in the room, the coach has been helping Philip get ready for an upcoming dance competition. 'You've gotten so much better this week.'

'But what did I miss? I feel like I messed up somewhere,' Philip says.

'There are a few rough spots in the middle segment.' The AI coach starts the music. 'Let's go back and try again.'

Meanwhile, across the ocean, Alisha in Melbourne, Australia wakes up one morning and doesn't feel well. Her throat is scratchy, she feels tired and her head hurts. Is it a cold? Flu? COVID? She doesn't know. So she rolls over in bed and talks to her AI health nurse. Like Philip's AI coach, the technology in her room allows the nurse to have a conversation with Alisha about her body and what might be making her feel unwell.

Have you ever wanted to get really good, even extraordinary, at something? Maybe it's dance or chess or cooking. It doesn't matter what it is; if you want to learn a new skill or foster your talent at something, AI will be able to help.

We want to be excellent. It's a very personal thing for each and every one of us, and it's terribly important to who we are as individuals.

AI will help with that. We will have personal assistants or coaches who can help each of us fulfil our secret dreams. It's hard to talk to other people about your dream to be something. It will be much easier to talk to your AI coach. You can work on that secret desire to be a great dancer or fantastic public speaker in the safety and privacy of your room BEFORE you reveal your awesomeness to the rest of the world.

AI will be a safe and fun way to explore who you want to be in the future and then it can coach you and help you get there.

BECOMING EXTRAORDINARY

Today there are a lot of apps and websites that can teach you new skills and hobbies. There are social media feeds and videos to show you how to cook or do woodworking or build things. These are really great. But they aren't personal. They aren't about you and how you might learn. They also don't adapt to you as you are learning. That's all going to change in the future.

THE BEST OMELETTE IN THE WORLD

Let's say you want to learn how to be a chef. That's cool. There are a lot of shows with celebrity chefs who have restaurants and books, and they are kind of like rockstars. Maybe you don't want to be a chef – maybe you want to be the best dancer, artist or whatever. That's also great, but the chef example will show you my point and then you can apply it to your passion.

OK, back to being a chef.

To be a great chef there are so many things to learn. Chopping, preparing and measuring ingredients. How to properly cook different ingredients, various flavours and how they go together. It's really exciting and there so many interesting things to learn.

Many of the chefs I know say that one of the best things to learn to cook first is a perfect omelette. Most people think it's super simple, but really it takes a lot of skill. And learning that skill is where AI could help.

Instead of watching a video or reading a cookbook (which are both good), imagine if you had your own chef coach who could help you along every step of the way. Things like

selecting the correct pan, using the right fat to cook the eggs, how to beat them and the all-important skill – **flipping the omelette!**

You could learn all these things by watching a video. But an AI coach could help you make specific changes and improvements as you learn – while you are learning, in real time. Maybe you should use a smaller pan to cook the eggs. Maybe you should use butter instead of olive oil. (I'm not a chef, but these are things that my friends have told me.)

That's how AI could help you make the best omelette in the world or make you an excellent dancer or chess player. But there's one thing AI won't be able to do in the future – taste your amazing omelette. That's OK; that's when you know it's time to reveal to your family and friends how you have mastered the art of the egg. Go ahead – **let them taste it**.

A TRIP TO THE DOCTOR IN THE FUTURE

AI could not only help you personally become extraordinary at something, but it could also help you understand your own personal health when you are feeling unwell.

Most people go to the doctor when they are feeling unwell. Unlike our animal friends from the previous chapter, we can tell the doctor what we're feeling. But that doesn't mean that the doctor can know right away what's ailing us.

This is where AI comes in. And once again, it all comes back to data. The human eye of a doctor can't take in nearly as much data about a patient as a computer can. That's especially true with things that are happening inside the body, with organs like the heart, lungs and liver.

It's no wonder then that some of the most exciting developments in medical AI are happening in radiology. Radiologists are doctors who specialise in treating disease using computer images, like X-rays and ultrasounds. These may sound scary but they're ways for the radiologist to work with other doctors to get a better understanding of what is happening inside the body. They look at these images and try to figure out what's wrong with the patient. And they're able to save many lives. But AI-powered computers will do an even better job of analysing the image, because they can compare it with a massive amount of data, including the patient's own medical history and that of other people who had the same problem with their body. This is what's known in AI as **BIG DATA**. And it's only going to get better at helping doctors heal patients and cure serious diseases like cancer and diabetes.

QUICK TECH TAKE:
Big data

Big data refers to data sets that are too big to be processed by humans or even by basic data-processing computer software. Only AI software is powerful enough to make sense of big data, with the use of algorithms that give computers the ability to solve complex problems. When it comes to medical AI, big data consists of patient records, radiological scans, surgical videos, journal articles and more.

Being able to figure out what's wrong with their patients quickly and accurately will help doctors start treating them sooner and more effectively.

TREATING YOU BEFORE YOU GET SICK

But what if your doctor could start treating you **BEFORE** you get sick? What if, with the help of AI, they notice symptoms even before you feel any of the effects?

It's known as analysing patterns of health. In the future, AI will be able to see patterns in the data and spot potential problems that the doctor might not think to look for. There are already some virtual AI chatbot health assistants that can take in information about a patient and assess their condition based on available big data. A chatbot is a computer program that simulates human conversation, allowing people to interact with digital devices as if they were talking with a real person. In the future, these tools will have access to even more data and be able to personalise their answer to you.

Today, when people are worried there might be something wrong with them, they often search the internet for possible explanations (asking Dr Google, as it's known). This can lead to false alarms and misdiagnoses. There is also a lot of misinformation out there about human health, since people without proper medical training are trying to play the role of doctor. But an AI chatbot will do a much better job of pointing the patient in the right direction because it has access to so much more information. And that will help keep them healthy.

THE FUTURE: 24/7 MEDICAL CARE

Once the doctor sends you home with your treatment plan, they can't be with you all the time – 24/7, or twenty-four hours a day, seven days a week. They have other patients to see and a family to have dinner with.

In the future, AI medical assistants on your phone or in your home (we'll talk about this in a later chapter) could be around when your doctor can't be, keeping an eye on your progress and making sure that the treatments are working. This is sometimes referred to as hospital-at-home technology.

Most importantly, the AI assistant of the future could be able to recognise when something bad is going on the moment it starts to happen. By analysing all the big data about your health, the software could predict the probability that you MIGHT get a certain condition or illness.

If that happens, it might start monitoring different vital signs to make sure that if something does start to go wrong, the doctor can be alerted immediately. That means help can arrive at the earliest possible moment, greatly increasing the odds of getting better.

Patient confidentiality

In the age of AI and big data, it's more important than ever to make sure that a person's medical information remains private. This is a big challenge for the healthcare industry. One solution that is being worked on is the 'de-identification' of a patient's information before it enters any AI database. This basically makes the data anonymous, so that anyone (or any machine) looking at it could never be able to trace it back to a single individual.

TAKING CARE OF YOUR MENTAL HEALTH

Getting sick is never easy and can take a toll on your mental health. AI has the power to make sure not just your body is healthy, but your mind and mental health as well. How you **FEEL** is important.

AI could also work with you and your doctor to get a better idea of how you are feeling and what might help relieve your anxiety. What's interesting about this kind of AI is that the software could be used on lots of different kinds of hardware. Remember, hardware is the physical place where the AI software can interact with you. Maybe that's your phone or the walls of your room. But in the future, it could be your bedside lamp or a favourite teddy bear. AI could be on anything that you feel comfortable talking to, which is especially helpful when it comes to your mental health.

In the future, AI could help us become even more extraordinary. That could mean learning a new skill or hobby or it could mean helping you feel better when you are feeling unwell and connecting you with the right healthcare professional, so that you can be the best person you **want** to be and the healthiest person you **can** be.

CHAPTER 6

▱ ✕

uploading . . .

Let's go inside your sentient home

ok

A VISION OF THE FUTURE . . .

In the suburbs outside Shanghai, China, two teenage sisters arrive home from school. As they walk up the front path, a hidden camera recognises their faces and automatically unlocks and opens the door. Once they get inside, the lights turn on and their favourite music starts playing through speakers in the walls and ceilings. They tell the home's digital assistant to ring a close friend and a few seconds

*later their face appears
on a monitor projected on to a wall.
They all chat for a few minutes, but then the
girls' mum pops on to the monitor and tells
them it's time to do their homework. She adds
that she's making one of their new favourites for
dinner, a meal recommended by AI based on all
the other food they've liked in recent months.
The girls clap happily and get down to
their homework.*

Like most sci-fi nerds, I love the word 'sentient'. It means the ability to 'perceive' or make sense of the world around you and take action in it. It often refers to creatures – dolphins and dogs are both described as sentient – they're so dang funny and smart. Robots can be sentient even if they are not conscious like you and me. Cars, too. And the technology is now reaching the point where entire homes can achieve a state of sentience.

Have you ever heard the saying, 'If these walls could talk . . .'? Thanks to AI, now they can!

Let's unpack this some more.

If you've ever used a digital assistant like Siri or Alexa, you've experienced AI. In the home, these digital assistants started out in Wi-Fi-connected speakers that are powered by AI software, with access to large amounts of data. When you ask them a question (What's the weather? How long will it take to drive to school today? Who is the greatest footballer of all time?), the assistant searches the vast trove of data and information for patterns and probabilities to arrive at the best possible answer. It's the same thing that's behind the palaeontologist identifying dinosaur footprints or a veterinarian diagnosing different animal conditions.

WHAT IS A SMART HOME?

We're now at the point where AI isn't only found in smart speakers and other gadgets. It's being built into the actual structure of some newer homes. You sometimes hear this referred to as the smart home. A smart home is a term that people use for homes that are filled with technology such as special sensors behind walls, inside appliances like the fridge and oven, and in the plumbing and heating systems.

All of these 'smart' devices are not only doing their primary job, like keeping the milk in the fridge cold, but they are also capturing all kinds of data about the home. Today people use these to control their gadgets remotely and automate functions like switching the lights on or off at a certain time.

Thanks to AI, smart homes will become sentient homes in the future. Instead of just having a bunch of devices simply connected to the internet, with AI, all of these devices will be talking to each other, collaborating and taking all that information to do things *on their own*. In the future you won't have to tell the devices to do something. Co-ordinated by AI, they will take care of the home, for example by shutting off the water if a leak is detected or turning up the temperature if the home feels a bit chilly. This is how the smart home is **STARTING** to turn into the sentient home. But a sentient home is more than that. In the future it could also understand you as an individual, connect you to other people and even keep you healthy (as mentioned in chapter 5).

ASK THE EXPERT:

Radha Mistry,
futurist, designer and professor

Radha Mistry is a futurist, designer and professor. She helps her students and architects and engineers, people who actually build homes and skyscrapers and roads and cities, to think about the future.

In the future, your AI-powered home will be your collaborator. It will connect you with friends, family, the city around you and most importantly your community.

As architects we are striving to make homes so that they can adapt and change to make people's lives better. AI will help with that. Imagine if your home could help you get up, get ready for school and make sure you had juice in the refrigerator for breakfast. Wouldn't it be amazing if AI could physically change your surroundings depending on what you needed to do? When it's time to do your homework, your *desk comes out, it gets quiet and the lighting is perfect for concentrating. When it's time to relax, your favourite music plays and the colours on the walls change. There's so much we'll be able to do.*

IF WALLS COULD TALK . . . AND WE COULD TALK BACK

In the future, you might even be able to have conversations with your home using a **chatbot**.

So why would we want to have a sentient home and walls that can talk (aside from your home being able to tell you jokes when you are having a bad day)?

KNOCK KNOCK

There are plenty of good reasons to have a sentient home.

MYTH BUSTER

The Myth: AI lets hackers into the home.

The Truth: While it's true that any Wi-Fi-connected device can be a way in for hackers, there are plenty of ways to keep them out – the same way locking doors and windows defends against burglars. For starters, all connected devices need to have a **'strong'** password, or one that is impossible for hackers to figure out, as opposed to **'1234'** or **'password'** (believe me, some people use them both!). Or you can use a password manager. That's an application that helps to manage all your passwords on all of your devices and accounts, leaving you to just remember one. In the future your password manager might use the shape of your face or the exact pattern of the iris of your eye to keep your passwords more secure.

Finally, you can also help protect your home by telling your parents or caregivers to check that your home's Wi-Fi router and other internet-connected devices are up to date, with all the latest security features and fixes.

IT HELPS THE PLANET

Unless you've been living under a rock, I'll bet you're hearing a lot about climate change. It might be the one topic that's even hotter than AI! The issue can get a little political, but if there's one thing most people agree on, it's that we should all try to use as little energy as possible, especially the kind that comes from sources which release harmful emissions, like oil and gas.

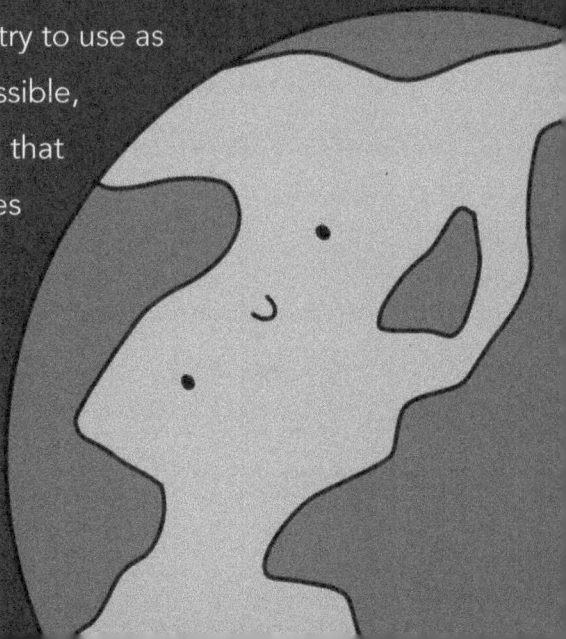

Did you know that homes use a lot of this energy? It's true! Our homes account for about **20% of the world's energy consumption.**

It doesn't have to be that way.

And AI can help!

Here's how . . .

00011010110

Homes produce a lot of data, and they react to a lot of data too. If you've learned anything by now, it's that there's one thing AI loves, and that's data. **Lots and lots of data!**

One of the biggest data sets has to do with energy. In the summer, a home uses energy to stay cool. In the winter, it uses energy to keep warm. It does this mainly by kicking on its heating and cooling equipment. But there are lots of factors involved, including the outside temperature, how many people are in the home (and which rooms they are using the most), the cost of fuel and electricity and even the temperature preferences of the people who live there.

What if there was a way to crunch all that data so that your home never worked any harder than it needed to keep you and your family comfortable? Thanks to machine learning, a smart home can already do just that. Its thermostats, for example, know to adjust the temperature when you're away or asleep.

Window shades go up and down automatically to either let sun in or block it out, depending on the time of year. If the home has rooftop solar panels, it can generate and store its own energy, and maybe even share it with the neighbours.

Here's the best part:

Saving energy saves money too.

When you add up all these AI-assisted changes, people with sentient homes could save hundreds of pounds on their annual energy bill every year and could spend it on fun stuff instead. Wahoo!

IT MAKES THE HOME A SAFER PLACE

When I was a kid, I liked being home alone. But a small part of me couldn't wait for my parents to get back, since it could be a little scary there all by myself. Maybe you feel the same way?

Well, AI can also be used to keep us safe and secure at home. Remember how AI can keep an eye on endangered animals 24/7? It could do the same thing with your home, using cameras equipped with two-way communication. AI can also get to know what you look like and the sound of your voice using **face and voice recognition**. By using this, it could get to know you and the other people in your life, like your friends and family. Who's that at your front door? Is it your best friend popping over to see if you want to go on a bike ride? Or is it a burglar trying to commit a crime?

Through **advanced diagnostics**, your home could also protect you from fires, floods and other catastrophes. In fact, some of this is happening already. For example, there are already sensors that can sync with a home's electrical wiring where they can detect dangerous sparking and defective appliances, both of which can lead to fires. Tiny, inexpensive sensors can also be placed in your home's water lines, alerting you to leaks, frozen pipes and other plumbing-related dangers.

IT MAKES LIFE EASIER – AND MORE FUN

But most importantly, the sentient home is also more fun to be in! In the future, when AI is in practically every home, it will get to know the people who live there even better. When you get home every day, the built-in AI could be ready to serve – streaming your favourite music, setting the lights and temperature to just the right level, helping with your homework (more on this later in the book) and coming up with a few ideas for dinner. If you had a tough day, it might even be able to tell that and then cheer you up with a few funny jokes.

This all sounds pretty good, right? But there are some down sides. We do need to be careful when we let computer systems with cameras, sensors and AI into our homes. AI might be nothing more than computer software, but many people have concerns about so much monitoring going on in the home.

It will be important for anyone who has a sentient home (or even just a smart one) to have total control over their data and systems.

There are simple steps you can take today, like talking to your parent, caregiver or teacher about what data to keep personal and what is all right to share. If something doesn't feel right in a chat room, game or email – for example, you're being asked for your personal information – **don't engage with that person**. Get an adult and tell them what's worrying you. Being aware of your privacy and data is a great first step.

In the future, your home will still be **your** home. You will want it to be comfortable and safe. The **goal** of AI is to make it a little **more** comfortable and safe, as well as more planet-friendly and just plain fun.

CHAPTER 7 ⊘ ☒

uploading . . .

Robots! Drones! And the machines of the future!

ok

A VISION OF THE FUTURE . . .

In Dublin, Ireland, Paul comes home from school and walks through the front door. Jimmy, his robot, walks from the front room. 'Hello, Paul! How was school?' the robot asks. 'Not great.' Paul slips off his backpack and tosses it on the floor. 'I got a bad mark on my maths test.' Jimmy walks over to Paul and looks up at him. 'I'm sorry about that,' he replies. 'Maybe we can work on a retest later, but how about we play a game now to get your mind off it? I'm still beating you at Space Pilot!' Paul smiles at the little robot, who has always been competitive. 'Sure, Jimmy, let's play a game.'

Across the globe, traffic is moving swiftly on the main highway leading into Buenos Aires, Argentina's bustling capital. A lorry carrying fresh produce from the country winds its way towards the city. Suddenly, a wild horse bolts on to the road. The lorry slams on its breaks, narrowly missing the animal. It's an impressive display of driving. But wait! There's no driver at the steering wheel. In fact, there's no steering wheel. The lorry is driving itself. It continues on its journey, right into the city centre, meeting little traffic on the way. That's because most of the vehicles on the road are self-driving, so there's little need for stop signs and traffic lights. In this driverless car of the future, traffic jams are a thing of the past – and so are blaring car horns!

Have you ever wanted to have your own robot? **I have!** My robot's name is Jimmy. He lives in my library. He's a cute and funny little guy. He's good at telling bad jokes and I like bad jokes! He's designed to be social, to talk and interact with people. He's only about a metre tall and was made to not be scary at all. I created Jimmy a few years ago with a team of designers, engineering friends and AI software designers. I know that AI and robots go together like peanut butter and jelly. They have been an important mix since robots were invented.

DID YOU KNOW?

The earliest robots as we know them were created in the early 1950s by George C. Devol, an inventor from Louisville, Kentucky. He invented and patented a reprogrammable

manipulator called 'Unimate', which comes from 'universal automation'. He tried to sell his product over the next decade, but it didn't take off. In the late 1960s, businessman and engineer Joseph Engelberger acquired Devol's robot patent and was able to modify it into an industrial robot and form a company called Unimation to produce and market the robots. For his efforts and successes, Engelberger is known in the industry as 'the Father of Robotics'.

SOFTWARE + HARDWARE = ROBOT

As we know, AI is software. It forms 50% of what makes up a robot. The other 50% is hardware (which we talked about earlier in the book). The hardware of a robot includes not only the microprocessors and visual sensors that help it understand the world around it, but also motors and special location sensors that help it move

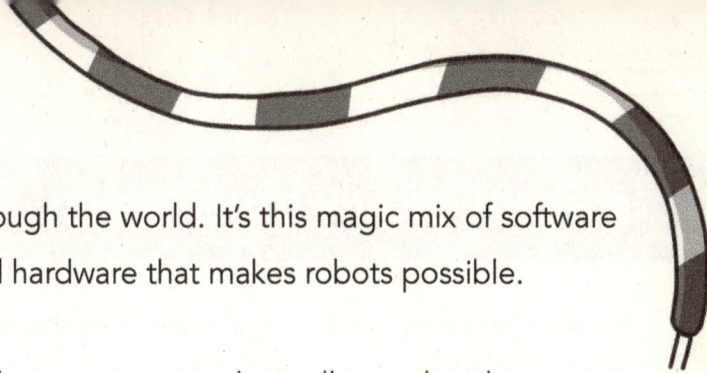

through the world. It's this magic mix of software and hardware that makes robots possible.

Today, we can see robots all over the place. Many of these robots are doing things that are difficult or hard for humans to do (like our underwater robots in chapter 2). Robots do things that are too dull, dirty and dangerous for humans. We call them the 'three Ds of robotics'. This is why we see robots at the bottom of the ocean, and why we find them in manufacturing plants building cars and in warehouses fulfilling online orders to be shipped to our homes.

The AI software on these robots enables them to perform specific tasks that they have been trained to do, like welding pieces of metal or pulling a specific product off a shelf and getting it ready for delivery. In fact, robots are one of the best examples of AI in action.

A ROBOT BY ANY OTHER NAME . . .

As we now know, a robot is a mix of AI software and hardware. This means that it can be a lot more than a robot in a factory or your robot friend that you play computer games with. Robots can go by many other names. A drone is a robot that flies around. A self-driving car is a robot that carries people around. A self-driving lorry is a robot that drives goods like food and trainers around. In short, a robot can go by many other names . . . but it is still a robot and it's powered by AI.

ROBOTS IN THE AIR: DRONES

We've already talked about UUVs – unmanned underwater vehicles. Drones are an example of UAVs – unmanned air vehicles – so instead of being down in the ocean, they're up in the sky.

Drones can be used in search and rescue missions, say if a hiker goes missing in the remote wilderness. Drones can be used to fight wildfires. And they're great for taking cool aerial pictures and videos. They can deliver medicine and supplies to people who are experiencing natural disasters. They can even be used for art, to create amazing shows in the air.

But we've only just scratched the surface when it comes to the potential of drones to change the world. Powered by AI, drones of the future could share data with one another, creating a worldwide network for moving around objects and people like never before.

What would you use a robot for, if it could travel through the air?

MACHINES OF THE FUTURE

ROBOTS ON THE GROUND:
SELF-DRIVING VEHICLES

Earlier in the book, we looked at how technology has accelerated our ability to get from point A to B by a whopping 10,000%. That's a rather dramatic change, but it's nothing compared to the impact AI will have on the transportation industry as a whole.

For many people, the idea of pulling out their phone and ordering a driverless car to take them to the shops or work seems like something out of a sci-fi movie. Since the beginning of transportation, humans have always been at the centre of the action. Bikes had riders, cars and trains had drivers, planes had pilots and so on.

One of the biggest effects AI is already having on transportation is the arrival of autonomous (aka self-driving) vehicles. Cars and lorries that drive themselves are REAL. In fact, they're already being tested on city streets all over the world!

FIVE CITIES WITH SELF-DRIVING CARS

- ✿ Ann Arbor, Michigan, USA
- ✿ Buenos Aires, Argentina
- ✿ Paris, France
- ✿ Pittsburgh, Pennsylvania, USA
- ✿ San Francisco, California, USA

This concept is a **BIG** leap for many people. Remember, it's human nature to want to be in control. This is why so many people are afraid of flying in a plane – they're not in control of the plane; the pilot is. It's one thing to put your faith in a pilot, since most regular people have no idea how to fly a plane. But at least there's a human in the cockpit (though as we'll see in a bit, that could change too!).

Driving a car is a different story. You're used to seeing your mum or dad in the driver's seat, or your friend's mum or dad. And they're *definitely* used to seeing themselves in the driver's seat. Now, all of a sudden, they're expected to trust a computer to drive the car? It's really too scary for some grown-ups to handle.

Don't get me wrong, there are still things that need to be worked out about the technology, which is why it's being introduced very, very slowly. Truly autonomous vehicles aren't widely used yet, but they are improving all the time. And as with the other AI-delivered changes to our world which we've covered in this book, that's a very good thing.

Why? I'm glad you asked!

DID YOU KNOW?

The first model of a self-driving car was revealed by General Motors at the 1939 World's Fair in New York City. The electric vehicle was guided by radio-controlled electromagnetic fields. It took twenty years for the concept to become a reality. In the decades since, engineers have continued to improve self-driving cars and there are even some on the road today – but they're not yet ready to replace human drivers completely!

SAFER FOR PEOPLE

AI-driven cars don't get distracted. They don't eat while they drive. They don't check their phones or fight with their sister or brother. They don't get sleepy or lost in daydreams. And they certainly don't take their eyes off the road while singing their favourite pop song at the top of their lungs.

Computers pay attention because that's what we program them to do – pay attention to every little thing happening around them. That means following speed limits and other rules of the road (which a lot of human drivers fail to do). It means noticing hazardous conditions, like slick surfaces or an object on the road (again, the kind of thing a lot of people might miss). It means always playing defence while driving by watching other drivers on the road (yep, one more thing we humans don't always excel at).

Equipped with AI camera technology and advanced sensors, self-driving cars will be able to take in all this information and more – trillions of bytes of data over the course of a single trip. It's like the AI computer back in *Space Pilot*, easily navigating the alien planet that no human pilot could possibly handle. To do this, engineers use a technology called **deep learning** to teach the AI what it should and shouldn't do in any and every possible situation.

QUICK TECH TAKE:

Deep learning

Deep learning is a type of machine learning that teaches AI to learn from examples, and it's based on how the neurons in our brains work. The main algorithms used in deep learning are called neural networks. They pass through different layers of information to help the AI work out what something is. For example, an AI using deep learning will look at an object it wants to identify, and it will recognise different features about it. In the next layer it will look more closely at just the features that it recognises, and will work out more about them. In each layer it gets closer and closer to the right answer. Using deep learning algorithms, the AI can learn which features are more important than others. This lets it look at the more important ones first so that it gets the right answer in fewer steps.

It works like this. Imagine you are looking out a window and you see something move. To figure out what you just saw, your brain goes through a rapid series of questions and decisions. Like this:

Is what I just saw an animal or a tree?
o **It's an animal**

OK, now I know it's an animal.
Is it a squirrel, a cat or a dog?
o **It's a dog**

So now that I know it's a dog.
Is it a poodle, a Great Dane, or a terrier?
o **It's a poodle**

OK, a poodle!
Is the poodle black or white?
o **Black**

So is it my black poodle
or is it another black poodle?
o **Yes, it's Franklin!**

Oh no, the dog has gotten out!

Deep learning follows a similar path by trying to understand data it is given that initially it doesn't know anything about. It allows the computer to ask a series of questions and make decisions to get to an answer with a high probability for being correct.

BETTER FOR THE PLANET

It's likely that self-driving vehicles will also be much better for the environment. For starters, they're going to be mostly electric, running on battery power instead of carbon-emitting petrol. Because computers are such safe, smooth drivers (no fast, power-draining accelerations, for example), autonomous vehicles could also operate more efficiently.

Since self-driving cars don't require human drivers, there could be a lot more ride-sharing services in the future. Everyone needs to go from one place to another, but not everyone needs to own a car. With fleets of self-driving cars on the streets, getting where you want to go could be as easy as pulling out your phone and ordering a ride.

That leads to another benefit of self-driving cars – the reduction in traffic.

A FUTURE WITHOUT TRAFFIC LIGHTS

Let's imagine what cars and buses and lorries of the future might look like if there are no human drivers. From the beginning, these machines were designed to have people driving them. With AI taking the wheel, can you imagine how these machines of the future might change? Maybe the front seat will disappear completely. Lorries won't need a cabin or place for the driver to sleep.

We don't have to stop at how vehicles will change. Imagine how the roads will be different. Would you need stop signs? Why would a super-connected car with AI and a vast sensor and data network need a traffic light? All the cars and vehicles would know where all the other vehicles are. They would all be connected. It would be like a perfectly choreographed ballet where all the dancers know exactly what the other dancers are going to do.

Beautiful and amazing!

ROBOTS MOVING STUFF

Robots wouldn't just carry people, either. They could carry things like trainers for your local high street shop or food for the grocery store.

This would change how we get things and where they are stored.

Imagine a large city like London or Paris. In the future, lorries filled with trainers and food could be moving around the city all the time. Connected to the AI network, they could be communicating with each other AND with the high street shops that are selling the goods. So there would be no need to store goods in a warehouse. In fact, the trainers on the lorry might not even need to go to the high street. They could come directly to you!

ROBOTS, ROBOTS EVERYWHERE

Earlier, I compared self-driving cars to a well-choreographed ballet. It's the same with drones, only on a much bigger scale. Drones can be big or small. They can fly over the ocean or land. And like autonomous vehicles, they don't get distracted and they never need a lunch break.

People will be able to program AI-powered drones, as well as autonomous cars and lorries on the roads below, to find the best routes for moving people and stuff around the world safely and efficiently. The best part about that? It means we humans won't have to work nearly as hard moving these things ourselves.

The future of robots depends on not just science and engineering but also creativity and imagination. There is no limit to what these robots on land, sea and air can do. So that means we need to imagine what new and amazing things we want them to do.

What problems would you solve?

How would you use robots in your town or community to make life better for people?

ASK THE EXPERT:

Eneni Bambara-Abban,
robotics engineer, STEM educator,
philanthropist and filmmaker

Eneni is a multi-award-winning robotics engineer, STEM educator, philanthropist and filmmaker.

When you think about the future of AI and robots, the possibilities are endless.

Imagine sports equipment that adapts to your style – like magical sneakers that help you run faster or a basketball that always bounces back to you. AI could make sports gear feel tailor-made just for you, making every game an even more incredible wild adventure.

In the future, AI will allow anyone to be a technologist. Maybe you don't have the access or the schooling, but as long as you have passion and a dream, you can still build amazing things.

As a roboticist, I tell people to not be afraid that your idea is too silly or small or far-fetched. We need all those ideas to make a really interesting future for AI and robots.

And getting started isn't hard. First you need to imagine it, and the more individual and unique the better. You can start putting things together that no one has ever thought of before; that's how we come up with new ideas. Even if it fails, try again! That's the beauty of engineering; even our failures teach us new things!

I'm just so excited about the future of AI and robots. My strongest advice to anyone is to keep building. Keep building robots. Keep building new ideas. Keep building your confidence. Keep building friendships with people who also like to make things.
Keep building.

CHAPTER 8

uploading . . .

Let's go to space!

ok

A VISION OF THE FUTURE . . .

The spacecraft makes a slow, circular descent to the red planet's space station. Fifty years have passed since the first human colony was established on Mars. More than ten thousand people now live there, many of them space engineers who are busy mapping new parts of the universe. And there's a lot to see out there! Mars was just the beginning. Thanks to an AI-powered telescope set up on the planet, signs of intelligent life are being spotted in neighbouring galaxies all the time. After the spacecraft refuels on Mars, it will continue its journey through the cosmos. The discoveries it makes just might alter the course of human history, unlocking deeper mysteries of the universe in the process.

As you know by now, AI loves big stuff. The bigger the stuff, the more excited we get to use AI to make sense of it.

Well, outer space is big. I mean mind-blowingly big. Chew on this fact: it's 384,400 km to the moon, and that's our closest neighbour in space! If the moon is our neighbour, then our solar system is our neighbourhood. The edge of our solar system is the point where our sun stops being the greatest gravitational force affecting us. Because it's so far away, it's difficult to measure exactly where the edge of our neighbourhood is. Astronomers estimate that it's in an area that starts about two thousand times further from Earth than the sun. Now that's big!

What we call our solar system is really a planetary system. We call it a solar system because we are centred around our sun. But that's only **OUR** neighbourhood. There are tens to hundreds of billions of planetary systems or 'neighbourhoods' in our universe.

DID YOU KNOW?

The universe is all existing matter, energy and space. It started with the Big Bang about thirteen billion years ago and has been expanding ever since.

The universe is very large, and its vast darkness is filled with a whole lot of stuff including planets, black holes, stars and asteroids. It's impossible for humans to survive in space for very long. We were born on planet Earth. We're Earthlings! We need water, food, gravity and oxygen, to name a few of the more important things to our survival. And all of them are very hard to come by in space.

But we as humans still want to know what's out there, right? If there was only something that could help us in that quest. Something able to process massive amounts of data and information, without ever needing to take a breather or break for lunch. Something that wouldn't miss its family after months or even years away exploring the universe.

I'm kidding, of course. **That thing exists today, in the form of AI!**

MYTH BUSTER

The Myth: Robots will take over the world.

The Truth: This is sometimes referred to as AI's 'replacement myth', or the idea that AI-trained robots will take the place of humans. It's the premise of a lot of fun sci-fi movies and TV shows. But, in fact, it's a pure work of fiction, as made up as any story of aliens from outer space coming and taking over planet Earth. As we've now seen many times in the book, AI robots will be put to work doing stuff that we humans can't do on our own, like travelling to the bottom of the ocean or driving a lorry for twenty-four hours straight without taking any pit stops. In short: robots aren't going to replace us. They're going to make us better!

The people who design, develop and test rocket ships, satellites and other equipment used in space exploration are called aerospace engineers, though you might hear them referred to as rocket scientists. They're some of the smartest people in the world. But even rocket scientists can't figure out everything, which is one reason why, through decades of space exploration, we've only successfully landed humans on the moon and unmanned vehicles called Rovers on a couple of planets (Mars and Venus).

With the help of AI, there's the potential to do so much more. The technology is already being used to manage the complexity of a spacecraft's take-off and landing. It's also helping them dock safely at space stations. Rovers use AI constantly to help them drive around the surface of Mars on their own. And it's being used by people to help discover new planets and study the stars. Engineers and astronauts use a neural network (remember those from page 148?) to calculate larger distances and keep track of the locations of planets, asteroids and satellites.

THE SEARCH FOR INTELLIGENT LIFE

Of course, when it comes to space exploration, one of the most exciting things will be finding other forms of intelligent life. Most space scientists will tell you that, based on the sheer vastness of the universe, it's almost a certainty that other life is out there. Does that mean another planet like Earth, with a human population that looks just like ours? No, most likely it will be very different.

But AI is already helping us narrow down the possibilities. For more than a century, an international collective known as SETI (short for **'search for extra-terrestrial intelligence'**) has been on the hunt. The universe makes a lot of noise, so sorting through all the signals is a massive project. Volunteers from all over the world have helped over the years, but there's still too much data to process. Now it's not just radio signals. Telescopes are collecting millions upon millions of images too. In the future, AI will take all of this data, quickly sort through it and identify possible worlds where there might be life.

ASK THE EXPERT:

Beth Clarke,
astrophysicist and software engineer

The most exciting thing about AI is that it will allow us humans to explore other worlds that we haven't been able to touch yet. At the moment we can get to the moon; we've done that multiple times. We are going to get to Mars, I believe, in the next few decades. But if we want to explore the wider solar system, or other solar systems, and even other galaxies, which is really the rest of the universe, there are real limitations. As humans, we have the desire to get out into the universe, but we are going to need AI to do it.

THE FAR, FAR FUTURE: STEPPING INTO THE GREAT BEYOND

As we discussed, space is vast. It will take a long time for us to get to the edges of our solar system and beyond. But we will always want to go there. Humans are curious and we are explorers. We want to know what's over the horizon, what's 'out there'.

But we humans only live for a maximum of around a hundred years. If we wanted to live on other planets or meet other life forms, we would have to travel a really long way to even get close. This just isn't possible because of our human lifespan. The distance is too big and the time is too long.

But AI is a tool that could allow us to get further. On a futuristic spaceship, AI could monitor the people onboard and pilot the spaceship. AI might even help us get into a physical state where we could survive those long journeys and then extend humanity out into the greater reaches of the universe! Woah.

The idea of deep space exploration may seem like science fiction, but consider that AI is being used today to do things like navigate and dock spacecraft, to avoid things like planets, asteroids, satellites and all the other stuff in space. The next ten years of AI in space will be filled with opportunities. Remember our AI video game, *Space Pilot*? Human exploration of the universe will start to resemble that, since the farther we travel into the cosmos, the more 'unknowns' we are likely to encounter. We're going to need a lot of help from AI, whether it's designing new spaceships or helping us plan future missions.

SPACE HOOVERS: CLEANING UP SPACE JUNK

Did you know that space is full of junk? There is a ring of space junk that surrounds the Earth. It's filled with things like broken and old satellites and even a bag that was dropped by an astronaut while doing work on the International Space Station.

This junk is dangerous. When spacecraft and satellites and space stations need to move through this field of space junk, it can damage the craft. And as you know, that spacecraft or satellite is far away from Earth so we can't fix it like we can fix a car that drives over a nail on the road.

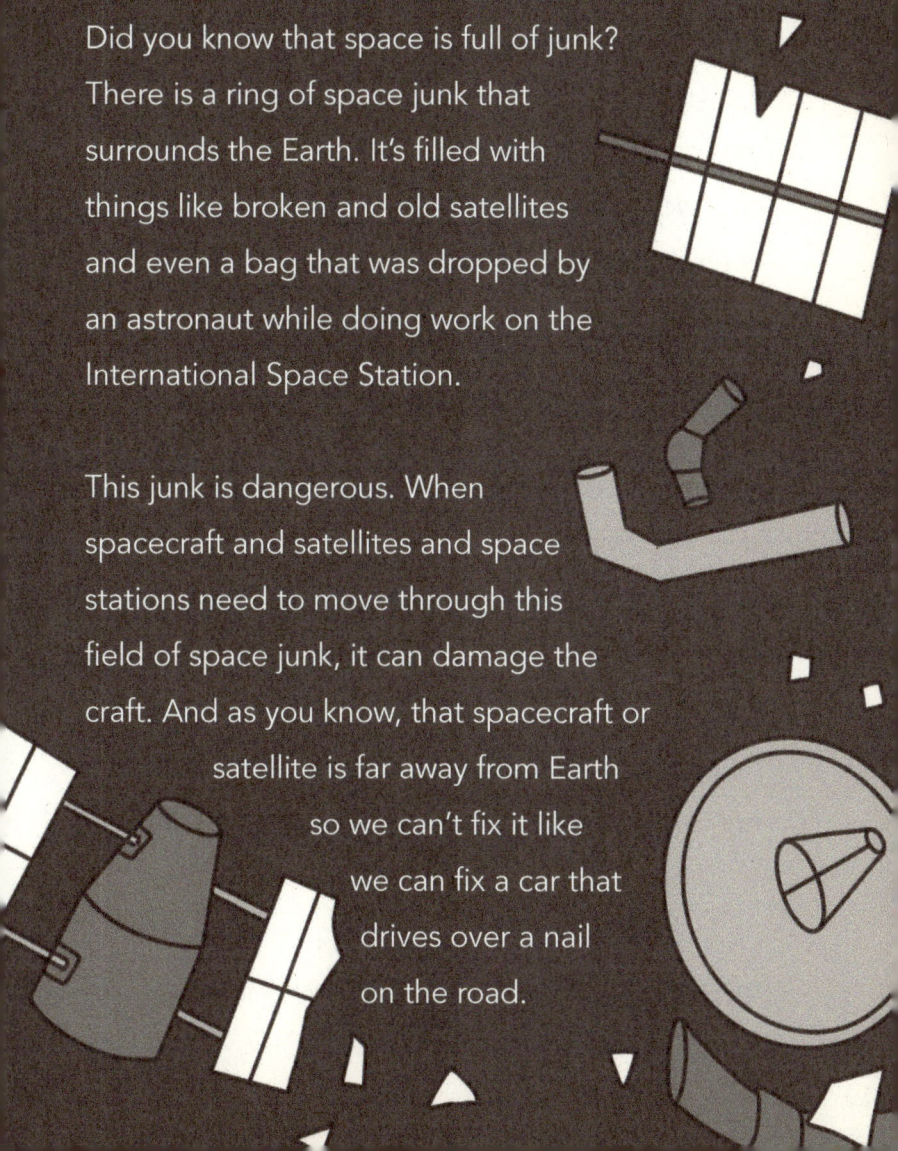

But with AI we could develop junk-removing satellites. These would be like space hoovers that travel through space, use AI to detect what is space junk and what is actually a working satellite. It could then suck up and remove the space junk, making space safer and clearer for all of us. How cool would that be! Maybe you'll be the person in control of this bit of tech, or even inventing it!

GREAT POSSIBILITIES

It's enough to make an astrophysicist's head spin! Fortunately, AI is now being put to good use, processing the images and sound signals. Using all the AI-related technologies we've talked about, from **big data** to **deep learning**, it's helping scientists zero in on the areas of outer space that are most likely to have intelligent life.

In short, AI will help us unravel and explore the mysteries of the universe. Now that is pretty cool!

CHAPTER 9 ▨ ⊗

uploading . . .

Unlimited creativity

ok

A VISION
OF THE FUTURE . . .

Alex in Bristol, England, has a great idea. She's not the best at drawing and she's too young to do industrial design, but . . . the idea itself is brilliant. She starts talking with her AI design software. She prompts the AI and it gives her some examples, but they aren't completely right. She keeps working with the AI to refine her idea. No one has ever seen this before. If you love panda bears, you are going to love what Alex has created . . .

I mean, really – who doesn't love getting creative? Do you like drawing? Painting? Movies? Music? Games? Since art is the process of creating, it can be almost anything! As we've seen repeatedly during this journey through AI, the technology loves big, vast, wide open areas of interest. And creativity clearly falls into that category. It can be *anything*? AI says, **'sign me up!'**

There are many ways that AI is influencing creativity. Technology and creativity have always crossed paths. But the relationship is often a tricky one, at least in the beginning. In the early days of photography, people said it wasn't a form of art, because they thought the camera was doing all the work. Today, photography is one of the purest art forms, because we understand that it starts with a human eye. Photography is a collaboration between people and machines.

QUICK TECH TAKE:

Generative AI

Generative AI is exactly what it sounds like. This might be the first time in our Quick Tech Takes that the term we are defining actually makes sense! Generative AI is AI that can generate an original response to your request. It is an amazing tool for humans to interact with AI. We simply ask the AI for something, and it gives us a response. Interacting with generative AI is often called prompt engineering – meaning that you prompt the AI (meaning ask it a question) and it gives you a response.

You might not have come across the term generative AI before, but I'll bet you've heard of some of its applications. Like ChatGPT? Or Google Bard? These AIs or chatbots are examples of generative AI that use natural language processing (we talked about this on page 80 and 82) to create all kinds of human-like content. They do this by using any digital content on the internet that's related to the topic you asked about.

For example, if you ask an AI chatbot to tell you who the best tennis player of all time is, it will analyse tons of data related to player stats, trophy winners and articles on tennis to come up with the best possible answer. AI doesn't get things right 100% of the time, though. AI is useful and helpful, but it could be looking at incorrect information. Always use common sense to check whether the AI is making sense.

AI chatbots have many uses, especially when it comes to creating content that doesn't require original reasoning, for example, summarising previous ideas or telling you how other people articulate an idea.

Of course, it can create other kinds of content. That's why generative AI and AI chatbots are so important to creativity. A chatbot could even write a short story if you asked it to. But that raises a lot of questions. Remember, AI is software that is trained by examples. I would have some questions about our short story-writing AI chatbot. For example . . . on what stories was it trained? Who wrote those stories? Did those authors give permission for the engineers to train the short story writing AI chatbot on their stories? This is a big one – it's really important for authors and other creators to say it's OK for their work to be used by AI systems.

I would also want to ask why you'd even want a story written by an AI, aside from it being an interesting experiment. Human original creativity is far more interesting. AI can only draw from content that already exists so it is only spitting out something that is like a mash-up of everything that has been fed into it. It doesn't come up with something that's 100% original. What you can create with your brain will be much more unique and brilliant.

That said, it can be helpful as a tool to inspire your creativity or unlock writer's block. For example, you might use an AI to give you a prompt for the setting of a story that you are going to write. If you haven't been there, the AI can do research and give you details about that place so that you can be creative and weave those details into your tale. Or you might be stuck writing a poem and finding it impossible to think of anything that rhymes with the word 'dinosaur'. Ask the AI chatbot for some rhymes, and suddenly you've got a dinosaur playing tug of war, on the seashore . . .

DID YOU KNOW?

Coding, or the writing of computer software, is a form of art too? When you write a computer program, like AI, you are being creative. You are making art. You are creating something out of nothing by using your imagination to come up with something new.

AI THAT CREATES . . . WITH YOUR CREATIVITY

We might not want AI to write us a story, but AI is great if you need help visualising your ideas. There are generative AI programs that allow you to 'prompt' AI to come up with new art that no one has ever created before. This is a great example of how AI and generative AI programs can be a tool for creative people to visualise things that they might not be able to draw or create on their own. It's not the ability to create the image that's important, but the emphasis is on the **idea** that **'prompts'** or gives the AI the raw material to come up with the amazing new visual.

ASK THE EXPERT:

Nicholas Nakadate,
designer, artist and 3D technical director

Nicholas is a designer, artist and animator who has worked on Hollywood movies like *Iron Man* and *Superman Returns*, designed trainers and created all kinds of art using AI. He's been doing it for over twenty years – and when it comes to AI, that's a really long time. Having used AI to design for so long, Nicholas has a clear understanding of what it means to art and creativity.

As an artist and designer, I have always used AI as a tool for my creativity.

The beauty of a tool like AI, when you use it for art and design, is that there are no limitations. You can imagine any crazy idea that you might have and you can make it happen. You can use an AI to combine things that might never go together like macaroni and cheese and a T. rex. You can tell it to design you a T. rex made out of mac and cheese and then animate it! It's unlimited creativity.

Maybe you don't like to draw or don't know how to animate. The AI can do that for you, but it still needs your creativity and big ideas. I like it because it lets me discover new concepts by combining things that don't go together. There are no limits for how it can be used as a tool for art.

AI FOR THE ART LOVER

It's not just artists who are playing around with AI in new ways. Art lovers can benefit from the technology too. One way is with the use of **art recommendation systems**. This is where an AI-enhanced computer recommends works of art based on a person's individual preferences.

You've probably seen this at work with music, where a streaming service suggests songs based on others that you've listened to recently. **It's the same thing with art.** That's good for the artists, since it exposes their work to a wider audience. And it's good for the art lover, since it introduces them to new artists.

WHAT IS ART? WHO IS AN ARTIST?

All that said, it's true that there is some controversy around the topic of AI and art. Many people who work in the arts worry that AI computers will take over their jobs. That includes illustrators who make their living drawing pictures, since a computer can do the work **faster** and **cheaper** than any human possibly can. Writers are worried too for the same reason. Even actors, since a computer can now come up with a 3D-animated version of any person on the planet and even mimic their voice.

AI is pushing us to re-examine what we think of as art, who the artist is and what creativity is. The truth is we don't know. It's up to us to decide what we define as art and who the artist is. This is not new. From photography to film, from digital designs to online art . . . the idea of creativity has always been challenged when a new tool is provided to creative people.

The real question is, what will you do with these new tools? **AND** what do you think is interesting and valuable?

AI = A TOOL FOR CREATIVITY

The most important point here is that, as I just mentioned, AI is a great mimic. It can recreate a piece of art based on data inputs that are fed into its software by people. It can produce a catchy jingle based on other examples that you give it. And yes, it can come up with its own version of a Hollywood star, modelled on real stars from the past.

What AI can't do is tap into the human emotion that's behind every great work of art. It can't draw on experiences from its life to write a beautiful poem or song. It can't find inspiration in nature by climbing a mountain or walking through a field of wildflowers.

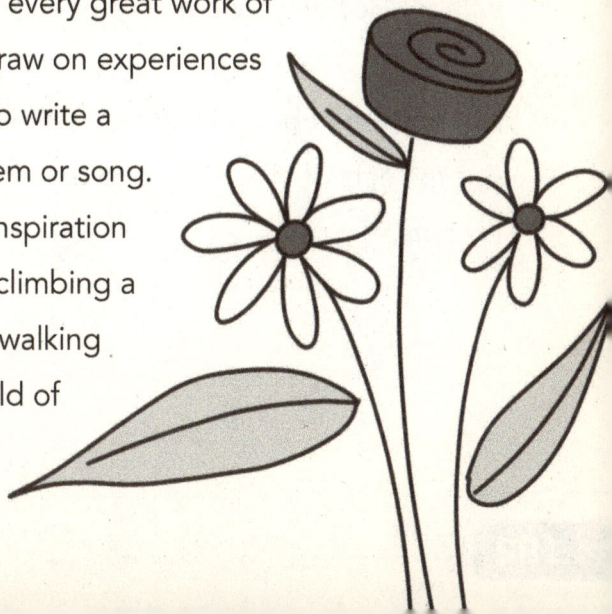

Only we humans can do these things. Art is about imagination, and that's why it will always belong to us. I like the example of David Hockney, one of the most influential artists of the twentieth and twenty-first centuries. The Englishman has always experimented with different technologies, from cameras to fax machines. In the 2010s, he started using his iPad to create amazing digital paintings. Then he brought in AI to make them even more original. These great works of art were helped along by AI. But they never would have been possible without Hockney's incredible genius.

Always remember: AI can help us make new art. But the acts of imagining and creating will always be ours.

QUICK TECH TAKE:

Deep fakes

Most of our Quick Tech Takes have been about exciting new technologies that are fuelling the amazing future of AI. But as with all tools, sometimes these amazing new technologies can be used for bad. Deep fakes are AI-generated videos and audio that can copy a person, usually a celebrity or politician, and make them say things in a video that they didn't say at all. At best these deep fakes can be fun having people say things that they would normally never say, but at their worst they can try to deceive you to think that someone you trust is saying something that they didn't say.

They best way to guard again the influence of deep fakes is to always check with your parents, a teacher or someone you trust to make sure that what you are seeing and hearing is actually true. But some of the tell-tale signs of a deep fake video are:

The background might be a bit blurry and the video pixelated

The facial movements of the person in the video will be a bit weird and unnatural, and their voice might be out of sync with their mouth movement

Too good to be true – if the person in the video is saying something too good, or just downright weird to be true, it's probably a fake

If it's from an unreliable website or untrustworthy social media platform, it's more likely to be fake

uploading . . .

Important stuff:

School and jobs

ok

A VISION
OF THE FUTURE . . .

At a school in a small, rural village in India, a teacher rings the bell that tells the students it's time to come to class. One by one, they file into the school and take their seats. Instead of pulling out pencils and paper for the day's lesson, they slip on virtual reality headsets. Each student meets with their private AI tutor for thirty minutes, where they get special instruction based on their individual needs. More maths problems for this student, an extra biology lesson for that one. Then it's time for a virtual class trip. Excitement fills the room. The kids have been looking forward to the trip for weeks. Moments later, they are in an AI-generated studio in Bollywood, learning the art of moviemaking from some of biggest actors and directors of the day! The class gets to make their own movie by just talking to the AI production software – that is, if they don't stop talking over each other!

What does AI mean for the future of school? Think back to the humble calculator – even though a calculator can help you do maths, that doesn't mean that learning how to do maths yourself isn't important. As we have seen throughout this book, AI is a tool that can be used by people, and in the future, children will use AI in school.

Now, there are some worries that students using AI to do their schoolwork will mean that they are not learning. But I don't agree with this. Students who use calculators are still learning in school, they are just learning differently from previous generations.

And that's the key to the future of AI and school and, eventually, jobs – we will need to learn differently, use new tools and develop new skills.

ASK THE EXPERT:

Andrew Maynard,
university professor and author

Andrew Maynard is a university professor and author who studies AI and the future. He teaches students how to use AI tools like ChatGPT or Google Bard in their schoolwork and jobs, so they can get ready for their future with AI.

AI is exciting because it will give students new opportunities in school and in the jobs they will get when they are older.

To use AI in the future, a student just needs four skills to do whatever they want to do with AI:

1. Be able to ask a good question
2. Listen and understand the answer to that question
3. Think about what your second or follow-up question should be
4. Be able to express yourself with language, meaning being able to take the thoughts in your head and turn them into spoken language that other people and AI can understand

In the future, nearly all of our interactions with computers and AI will be by just talking. That's why communication and self-expression are so important.

AI GOES TO SCHOOL

What happens when you take AI to school? Today you could use AI to write your next essay in history class or your next lab report in biology. But you really don't want to do that. Why, I hear you ask? Well, for starters, this kind of misses the whole point of school. You go to school to help you prepare for the future. School and your teachers help you learn how to think, ask questions and solve problems. AI doesn't do that. Actually, if you think about it, school teaches you how to **NOT** be an AI. It teaches you to ask questions and work with other people. It gives you the opportunity to share your **original** ideas and debate ideas with others. AI could be a helpful tool in school, but you will still need to be creative and inquisitive and collaborative.

And just so you know, yes, you can use AI to write your essay, but your teachers can also use

AI to check if your essay was written by you or an AI. In fact, they can usually tell if AI has written your homework anyway. As we've said before, AI is not human. If you have ever read anything produced by AI, you'll see that it often lacks personality. It's, well, a bit robotic. Teachers will be familiar with your *style* of writing, the typos you always make, the tone you write in, as well as the things you haven't been taught yet. It will be VERY obvious to them that AI has written your homework. Sorry, but it really isn't worth it!

AI TEACHING ASSISTANTS FOR TEACHERS AND YOU

OK, so we don't want AI to write your homework. But AI in the classroom is about more than just chatbots writing essays. In the future, technology is going to help students and teachers alike in ways that have nothing to do with generative content.

We've seen how AI makes for excellent assistants in other fields, from science to medicine. In the future, teachers could have their own AI assistants, freeing up so much time for teachers to do what they do best – help you learn! Teachers spend so much time on tedious tasks, like inputting grades and checking attendance. AI could do all this stuff in its sleep (well, it doesn't sleep, but you get the point). Very soon, AI software might even help grade papers, especially in subjects that involve a lot of numbers and data. But it won't replace the teacher, it will just be the first review of the paper and then the AI would pass its findings on to the teacher to make the final mark.

Then there are the AI assistants for students – basically private tutors designed just for you.

With access to your entire academic record, all the way back to your early school years, the tutor could be able to pick up on trends and patterns and give you support accordingly. If you were always good at maths, but suddenly you're struggling, the tutor might suggest some extra worksheets for you to practise with.

In the near future, your AI tutor could also help you map your academic future, even helping you find the perfect university, based on your grades, interests and extracurricular activities. Of course, the final decision would be yours. But as with everything in the future, AI will be there to make the experience that much better.

MYTH BUSTER

The Myth: AI machines will take over all the human jobs.

The Truth: There's a long history of technology being seen as a job killer. When Johannes Gutenberg, a German goldsmith, came out with the first printing press in 1436, people said it would mean the end of 'scribes', or workers who hand wrote books, pamphlets and other reading materials. That was partly true, but the printing press created so many other jobs, since it made it possible for practically everyone to learn to read. It's the same thing with AI. Unfortunately, some jobs that involve a lot of automation could go eventually. But AI technology will create so many new areas of human knowledge and discovery, including all the stuff we've been talking about in this book. In short: AI will lead to the creation of different jobs, ones that don't even exist today!

HOW TO PREPARE FOR YOUR FUTURE JOB

The rest of this book is going to focus on how to prepare for your future with AI (spoiler alert: it's exciting!).

But I wanted to talk about jobs and your future career. Now, parents, teachers and most adults like to talk a lot about jobs and your future. They are kind of obsessed with it. The reason they are so concerned about your **job** future is that they want you to be successful. They want you to be happy and have all the things in life that you need. That's not a bad thing, right? But it can be a lot of pressure.

You may not know what you want to do in the future (we'll talk about this again soon – I can help!) and that's OK. You have time to figure it out. You have time to change your mind. But if we want to get serious about your future and AI – and I'm guessing because you have read so far in this book that you are **super serious** – then, great, let's talk.

Your future will be completely different to the future that your parents experience – which is also known as today. You are going to need specific skills to succeed in your future and those skills are different to the ones people have been taught in the past. You are going to need to understand AI and explore how it might help you in the future (which you've already done by reading this book!). But you are also going to need to be more human. Your social and verbal skills will be very important. You are going to need to be able to talk and express your ideas.

You'll need to be able to have empathy so that you can get along with other people. You are going to need to be able to take your thoughts and communicate them to other people, and even to AI. If you can do that, you will be successful.

Our next step is to explore that future.

What does your future look like with AI?

AI and your future

Where we explore your future and AI,
how to imagine it and how to make it happen!

ok

What you need to know about AI – the secret revealed! (Did you skip ahead?)

The secret to knowing everything you need to know about AI is to **always be curious**. Always try to learn more. Always ask questions. Always be critical. You don't have to believe everything.

AND you know what?

You are always doing this! By reading this book you are actively being curious. You now know how to ask questions and look for answers.

The secret is . . . you are already prepared for the future. If you remain curious, you will always know everything you need to know about AI.*

ASK THE EXPERT:

Steve Brown,
futurist

Steve Brown is a futurist and friend of mine. He has worked with many AI and tech companies to get them prepared for the future of AI.

If you want to make sure you are successful with the future of AI, I'd say make sure you have good friendships.

*By the way, this works for almost everything in life. Be curious! Get excited!

It will, of course, be important to know a little bit about how AI works and what it can do, but what's more important is to make sure you have a life filled with good friends and that you spend time doing things you're passionate about. Have lots of hobbies. And when it comes to the future of AI, it's not really about AI . . . It's more about you and your life and how you will use these new AI tools to get through your day and to create amazing stuff. If you only focus on the technology, you're probably looking at the wrong thing. Remember . . . you are more important than any technology or AI.

AI AND YOUR FUTURE

We've spent our time together talking about what AI is and what it isn't. We have explored why so many people are talking about AI and why some people are worried about it.

We've taken a rollercoaster tour through all the ways that AI could make the cool things in your life even cooler. You'll be able to interact with dinos, excel at football and maybe even talk with your pet!

Now let's talk about your future. That's what I do as a futurist. When I talk with people about their future, I always ask them the same question first:

What is the future you want?

You MAY think that my question is kind of like the question that adults and teachers and people are always asking you: what do you want to be when you grow up?

But it's not. I don't like that question. I want you to be more specific.

Now that you have an understanding of what the future could look like and all of the amazing things that could happen – I want you to think about yourself.

What do you want to be in the future? Wait. That's too broad. Let's try this – what will a Tuesday be like in your future? What will it be like to wake up? What will your room look like? What will you have for breakfast?

I don't want to know what **job** you will have in the future. Tell me the kinds of things you want to **do**.

Who are the people you want to hang around with? Palaeontologists? Zoologists? Volcanologists? Footballers? Artists? Think about all the people we looked at in this book.

Maybe you'll hang out with more than just **PEOPLE**. Maybe furry friends or wild animals.

What will you have for lunch?
What will you do for fun?

I think you get the idea – it's not **what** do you want to do when you grow up. It's what do **you** want to do? Specifically. What are you interested in? What are the things in the previous chapters that you found interesting (great!)?

What did you find **NOT** interesting at all in the previous chapters (also great!)?

Often, it's more helpful to know what you don't want to do – what you are **NOT** interested in – because then that allows you to focus on what you **DO** want to do.

So do this thought experiment with me.

Tell me the story of the future you. Tell me in detail. Tell me about what you are interested in today. It's OK if it changes tomorrow – that's also a good thing, as you get a better understanding of what you want to do. Things change. You will change as you grow up.

What does the future hold?

Well, that's up to you.

Think about the future you want. Write it down on a piece of paper. Remember the questions we mentioned earlier – what will it be like to wake up in your future? Where will you live? What will you have for breakfast? Who are the people you will hang out with?

Then stop thinking about it. Go to school. Watch some telly. Have some breakfast. Play a game.

Then come back to it and see what you said. Do you still agree with it? Great! Keep going.

If not, then change it. Write it again. Great!

Why am I making you do this? Well, the future of AI is all about you. AI is just really interesting software that can do a specific set of things.

Now, granted, in that set number of things there are a lot of variations and possibilities and interesting things that AI can come up with that you didn't expect, BUT what AI can do is limited. But YOU are not limited. Your creativity, new ideas, sense of humour, sense of fashion and relationships with your friends are limitless.

What will make the future of AI interesting is **YOU**.

It's what you want to do with it that's important, and what you want to do with AI is tied directly to what **YOU** want to **DO**.

ADVICE ABOUT YOUR FUTURE

So, how could AI help you succeed in this future you have just mapped out, and how can you prepare for it?

Many people might tell you to learn to code. To learn how to program a computer. If you want to do that, **GREAT**!

But what if I told you that you could have an amazing future with the help of AI and you **DIDN'T** have to learn to code? **GULP** – this is a little strange for me, because I'm an engineer who loves to code, but go with me.

I want to tell you something new. Something people haven't told you yet.

OK, so . . . you don't have to learn to code or be an engineer to be successful in the future.

I'm saying this because **STEM** and AI will be a part of **EVERYTHING** you do in the future even if you don't learn to code.

Look at all the things we talked about in this book. If you want to be a …

Footballer – you will use AI
Volcanologist – you will use AI
Palaeontologist – you will use AI
Artist – you will use AI
Designer – you will use AI
Dancer – you will use AI

The list goes on and on. You get the idea.

So I guess that's the myth buster for your future and AI. You are going to use it even if you don't know you are using it. It will be a part of everything you do.

It's like using computers and the internet, even if you don't think about them or even if you don't want to use them – they're still a part of your life.

AND also it's not a big deal. I mean, don't get me wrong, the internet and computers are a big deal. They are really cool and it took a long time to create them.

But for **YOU** – you probably don't think that it's a mind-blowing experience going online and doing a search or playing a game or contacting a friend. Part of the secret of AI in the future is that it won't be as much of a big deal as people are making it today.

QUICK (FUTURE) TECH TAKE:
Artificial general intelligence

There are some advances in AI that haven't happened yet, but which people are already talking about. Some people are very worried about these advances, while others are extremely excited about them. It can be confusing.

The biggest advance that **HASN'T** happened yet is something called artificial general intelligence or AGI. AGI is a lot like all the different kinds of AI we have been exploring in this book, but the one really big difference is that AGI is as smart as or even smarter than human beings. The main worry about AGI is that it will get out of human control, start operating on its own and then harm people. But some people are excited about the new things that an AGI could come up with that we humans have never thought about. They say it will make our lives exponentially better than they are today.

Now, before you get too excited or worried, there is a huge debate over whether AGI is even *possible*. I spoke with one brain scientist who told me it would never happen because we humans don't even understand how our brains work, and if that's true, then we can never make a machine that's smarter than a human. Another computer scientist told me that we need to think about machine intelligence as something completely different to the kind of intelligence we humans have. And that if AGI happens, it won't be a threat, it will just be a machine that's smart in a **DIFFERENT** way to us.

But because AGI hasn't happened yet, we just don't know. It's an interesting space to keep an eye on as we move into the future, and now you know both sides of the debate.

ASK THE EXPERT:

Natalie Vanatta,
cyber security professional, United States Army officer, professor, author and algebraist

Natalie has one of the coolest titles ever – she's an algebraist! This means she's a mathematician who specialises in algebra. It also makes her really good at codes and cyber security. She works to keep people safe from the digital threats AI can create.

Any technology that can be used to do good things can also be used to do bad things.

AI is just the same. It can be used for good or bad. It depends upon how **PEOPLE** *use it and what they want it to do. They can use it to make the world better or they can use it to commit a crime or hurt people. But that shouldn't worry you. This isn't new. It's really like a car. People can use a car to get around, go to school, go* to the movies – all good things. People can also use a car as a getaway vehicle from a bank robbery. Or if they misuse the car, they might hit a person crossing the street and hurt them.

You see, the car isn't bad or good. It's how people use it. The important thing to know is that we have laws and rules for how people can use cars and if people don't follow those rules they get in trouble. It will be the same way with AI.

HOW TO PREPARE FOR THE FUTURE

So, what can you do to prepare for this inevitable future with AI? Well, the biggest step is to understand the fundamentals of what AI **is** and what it can **do.**

I have a secret for you. Because you have read the first ten chapters of this book, then you have already done that! You are already on the way to preparing for your future. With this knowledge – you may want to re-read it!

But you are already there.

So, what do you want to do? Whatever it is, however it changes in the future, you can be confident that you are grounded in the fundamentals of AI. You now know lots of examples of what AI will do in the future. And what AI **MIGHT** do.

You are ready.

I can't wait to see what you do!

ONE MORE THING

But wait – there's one more thing you need to do, and this is very important.

You need to help other people understand the future of AI. You now know what it is and what it can do and maybe what it **WILL** do. We also talked about why some people are worried about it.

I need you to help them to understand what the future of AI **COULD** be.

This is important.

The future depends on you.

No, really, I mean it. I'm a futurist – I know. That's why I wrote this book and why we're having this conversation right now. **You will help shape the future of AI.**

You will help other people understand the future of AI. You have that power. If you think about it, you are kind of like an AI superhero. But keep it a secret. That's what most superheroes do, right?

Because AI will be a part of nearly everything we do in the future, just like computers and the internet are today. Building a better future with AI means building a better future for us all. **For the planet!**

But remember to do good.

Build the future you want.

And always be human! AI is a tool, but nothing will ever match the creativity and ingenuity of the human brain.

complete

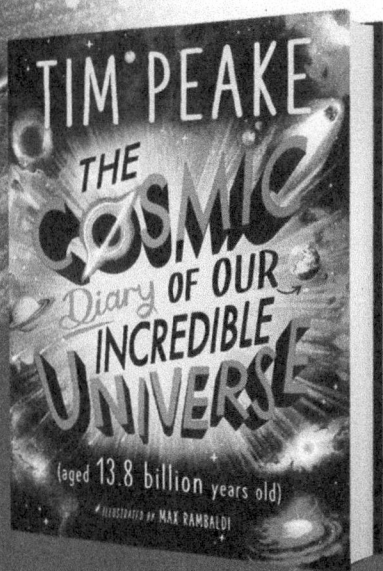

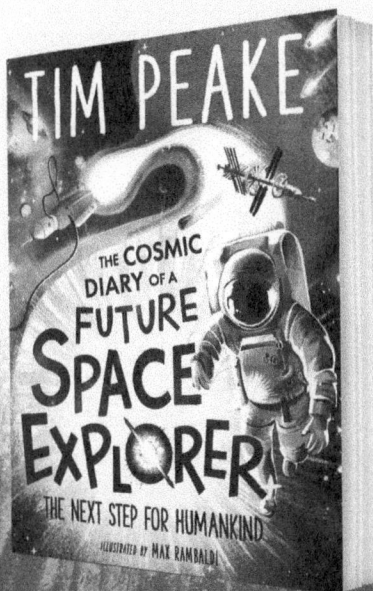

ACKNOWLEDGEMENTS ◪ ✗

Special thanks to my long-time collaborator Dan DiClerico for helping me noodle through the nuances of AI and figure out the best way to talk about its past, present and future.

Thank you to all the experts I interviewed for this book. A special thanks to those who were not highlighted in the Ask the Expert sections: Michelle McClure, Alisha Bhagat, Joshua 'Griz' Palochak, Cyndi Coon, Jason Brown, Josh Massad and Annette Aranda.

Thank you Laura Horsley for asking me.

Thank you to my parents, Jane and Dave; without them I would have nothing.

18
101
25

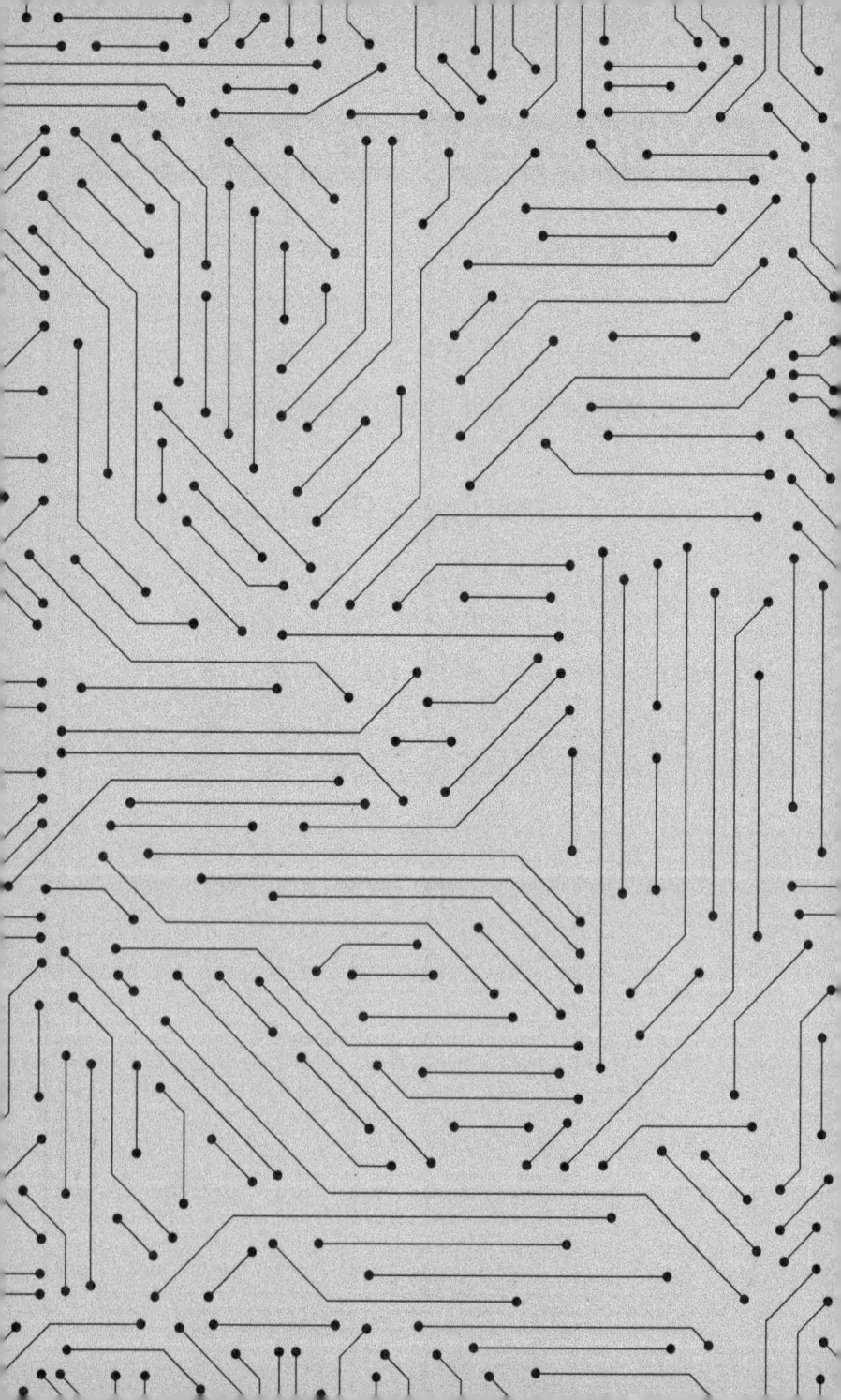